REPORTING FOR DUTY

True Stories of Wounded Veterans and Their Service Dogs

Tracy Libby

Reporting for Duty

Project Team
Editor: Amy Deputato
Copy Editor: Joann Woy
Design: Mary Ann Kahn
Index: Elizabeth Walker

i-5 PUBLISHING, LLC™
Chairman: David Fry
Chief Financial Officer: Nicole Fabian
Chief Digital Officer: Jennifer Black-Glover
Chief Marketing Officer: Beth Freeman Reynolds
Marketing Director: Will Holburn
General Manager, i-5 Press: Christopher Reggio
Art Director, i-5 Press: Mary Ann Kahn
Senior Editor, i-5 Press: Amy Deputato
Production Director: Laurie Panaggio
Production Manager: Jessica Jaensch

Library of Congress Cataloging-in-Publication Data
Libby, Tracy, 1958- author.
  Reporting for duty : true stories of wounded veterans and their service dogs / Tracy J. Libby.
     pages cm
  Includes index.
  ISBN 978-1-62008-198-3 (hardback)
  1. Service dogs--United States. 2. Disabled veterans--Services for--United States. 3. Animals--Therapeutic use--United States. 4. Human-animal relationships--United States. I. Title.
  HV1569.6.L53 2015
  362.4'048--dc23
                          2015024309

This book has been published with the intent to provide accurate and authoritative information in regard to the subject matter within. While every precaution has been taken in the preparation of this book, the author and publisher expressly disclaim any responsibility for any errors, omissions, or adverse effects arising from the use or application of the information contained herein.

i-5 Publishing, LLC™
www.facebook.com/i5press
www.i5publishing.com

Printed and bound in China
18 17 16 15   2 4 6 8 10 9 7 5 3 1

Dedication

To all of the wounded veterans, as well as active-duty soldiers, for their heroism and sacrifice, and to the canine heroes and their trainers who have helped change, improve, and save our veterans' lives.

Acknowledgments

Where do I start? So many professionals helped this book become a reality. What an unbelievable privilege it was to share these stories and to pay tribute to the canine heroes and brave soldiers who, according to them, "were just doing their jobs" (and would gladly do it again—even knowing the outcome).

First and foremost, thanks must go to the veterans who shared their stories with me so that I could share them with you, as well as the veterans who shared their time, experiences, and expertise so I could better understand military jargon and protocol. After more than thirty years of writing about dogs, I feel privileged to share the stories of fifteen wounded veterans and their canine heroes.

Hats off and a million thanks must also go to the professional photographers who generously donated their time and photographs, as well as to Colin Kimball for allowing us to use his Military Legacy Portrait of Michael Jernigan. You folks are the absolute best!

Much gratitude to the founders, presidents, CEOs, and volunteers of all of the service-dog organizations who generously shared their expertise, who put up with my pestering, and who worked so hard to put me in touch with our nation's heroes. You, too, are the absolute best!

I pitched this book to Christopher Reggio, i-5 Press's general manager, during an unrelated telephone conversation, and from day one his enthusiasm never wavered. He wholeheartedly backed this book and, in turn, put me in the hands of senior editor Amy Deputato, who has a keen eye for detail and the patience of Job.

Finally, a heartfelt thank you to my husband for pitching in with everything—including tons of proofreading—during the crazy, hectic, busy months of putting this book together as the ever-looming deadline rapidly approached.

My only regret is that I was unable to include more wounded warriors and their canine heroes. I hope the heroes profiled on these pages will speak for all of those who served and continue to serve our great country.

Foreword

I think you'll be moved by the inspirational stories of the veterans who have moved forward from injuries toward healthier lives with the help of service dogs. You'll read of their increased mental and physical activity, improved relationships with their families, greater engagements within their communities, motivation for compliance with treatment plans, and a decreased need for pharmaceuticals. Five of the profiles of veterans with service dogs in this book, *Reporting for Duty*, are from Veterans Moving Forward (VMF), the nonprofit organization that I cofounded with Bob Larson.

Just as there is no singular treatment plan that benefits all patients, there is no one model for obtaining, training, and placing a service dog with a disabled individual. Some of the organizations you'll read about in this book use rescued dogs; others have their own breeding programs. Some have civilian volunteer puppy-raisers who socialize and raise the puppies in their homes from eight weeks of age until the dogs return to their organizations' kennels and professional training staff at one year of age. Others use prisoners to train the puppies in basic obedience during the week and then use volunteer "puppy sitters" with whom the pups live on the weekends for socialization. Some organizations charge modest processing fees to the applicants, some expect a "pay-it-forward" fundraising campaign for the estimated value of a service dog, a few charge tens of thousands of dollars for fully trained service dogs, and others provide the service dogs to veterans at no cost.

I, too, like the veterans and canines in this book, reported for duty, first as an enlisted woman and officer who served honorably in the US Navy between 1977 and 2001 and then as a social entrepreneur who, in 2010, saw a need to help our nation's disabled veterans. I believed that I could make a difference in the lives of America's veterans based upon my professional background and my firsthand experience in raising, socializing, and training (for a well-established service-dog organization) an assistance dog. I witnessed the overwhelmingly positive difference that this puppy made in the mood, comfort, hopefulness, and deportment of the military personnel and veterans, their families, and their healthcare teams when I visited several military treatment facilities and medical centers of the Department of Veterans Affairs (VA). I knew that one dog could greatly benefit more than one person in the course of his training pipeline, and that's why I created a new model for VMF.

I also learned that the dogs could help select their disabled partners. I witnessed several of VMF's dogs appear indifferent to and unwilling to engage in play or polite people greetings with particular veteran candidates—even before the team of healthcare professionals and canine trainers gathered to conduct the formal interview with the veteran and his or her primary caregiver or partner. I don't know exactly what the dogs were reacting to—whether it was the individual's energy level, inability to be open and authentic, hesitancy to make a commitment to work toward recovery, or something else. I just learned to trust the process, which means both paying attention to what the dogs are telling us and following the guidance of VMF's behavioral healthcare specialists.

The veteran's hard work toward recovery begins in earnest upon being matched with a service dog in training. The amount of time required to learn what is necessary to pass the Public Access Test and be viewed as a solid service dog–veteran team varies widely. There is much for the veteran—even a previous dog owner—to learn. The process begins with the veteran's learning a new vocabulary

and the techniques used to train his or her dog to perform specific tasks to mitigate the individual's specific disabilities. The veteran learns how to properly groom and care for the particular dog, how to provide good nutrition, how to maintain the dog's health with preventive and veterinary care, and how to provide adequate rest, safe playtime, and daily exercise. Additionally, the veteran partner is what constitutes appropriate service-dog conduct and how to educate the public about service dogs in general as well as the specifics of the federal law known as the Americans with Disabilities Act (ADA).

The most significant characteristic of an effective service dog–veteran team is the relationship, which is built on mutual trust. In addition to learning how to trust each other, both entities need to learn how to read each other. By far, the dogs are better at the latter than the humans are. The dogs are such keen observers that they pick

up on very subtle cues and note changes in behavior patterns even before many of the veterans know that they are exhibiting any type of indicative behavior that something is amiss. The dogs are trained to offer behaviors in response to these indications, which in turn prompt the veterans to do something to mitigate their condition. These actions may be observed as the service dog retrieving medication, tugging on the veteran's sleeve, or pulling on the leash to prompt his partner to depart an area that may be causing increased anxiety or panic and seek a safer location. Other actions include the dog's licking the hand or face of the veteran in order to bring him or her back from a flashback, nightmare, or blackout. In any event, the veteran needs to trust and reward his or her service dog and take responsibility for moving forward toward recovery and a healthier life.

So, let's remember why all of these organizations voluntarily *reported for duty*—because the need is overwhelming! The US government—more specifically, the VA—is unable to meet the needs of its disabled veteran population. More than 540,000 veterans of the wars in Iraq and Afghanistan have PTSD and/or depression, and more than 260,000 veterans have been diagnosed with traumatic brain injuries (TBIs), according to a study done by the RAND Corporation in September 2014. Remember, these numbers, totaling close to one million veterans, do not count the veterans from other wars, from peacetime service, or with other physical injuries, illnesses, or diseases that could benefit from service dogs.

Therefore, even if each of the service-dog organizations currently operating in the United States increased its annual service-dog placement output by a factor of 100, we still collectively could not meet the needs of our nation's veterans who struggle with multiple health challenges. (Please note: As reported by the Federal Register, it is presently the policy of the VA to provide service dogs only to veterans with visual or hearing impairment or select mobility challenges.)

Read about these valiant veterans and first responders who are brave enough to seek help, to work diligently at creating solid relationships with their service dogs, to hide no longer, and to become visible in society again as they make remarkable progress in their recoveries. Learn more about these wonderful organizations that are helping the veterans like those profiled in *Reporting for Duty*…and *get involved!*

~ Karen D. Jeffries, Commander, US Navy, Retired
Cofounder and President Emeritus, Veterans Moving Forward, Inc.
Daily Points of Light Award winner

INTRODUCTION

For nearly thirty years, I have been writing about dogs—their history, their origins, and the purposes for which they were originally bred. I've covered canine nutrition, genetics, breed-specific diseases, and cutting-edge veterinary research, to name just a few. Yet I am endlessly curious about why we love dogs and why they love us unconditionally in return. Why we are eternally devoted to dogs? Why do we grieve so deeply when it's time to say good-bye? Do dogs grieve? These are among the thoughts rattling around in my brain at any given moment. My work has led me to some of the top researchers in the country, as well as to top-notch breeders, trainers, and behaviorists. I have met owners so devoted to and so bonded with their dogs that they are willing to give up nearly everything to protect them, to provide good veterinary care, and to ensure that their lives are comfortable.

While researching my last book, *The Rescued Dog Problem Solver*, which profiles twelve dogs who were abused, surrendered, abandoned, or otherwise forgotten but who, through human kindness, found loving homes and went on to excel as treasured companions, I came across a photograph of a disabled veteran in a grocery store with his rescued shelter dog. The dog, trained to provide help to individuals with post-traumatic stress disorder (PTSD), walked ahead of the veteran's wheelchair, searching the aisles and alerting to any potential threats. I was struck by this veteran's story and by his dog's training and devotion. Immediately, I wanted to know more about our nation's veterans and their specially trained service dogs.

In this book, you will meet fifteen veterans who unselfishly volunteered to protect our freedoms and, in doing so, paid an enormous price, as did their family members—husbands, wives, mothers, fathers, sons, daughters, brothers, and sisters. Fifteen veterans who agreed to share with me their stories of adversity, resilience, survival, triumph, and canine companionship so I could share them with you. Some of the veterans offered only brief descriptions of their military service. Understandably, they were reluctant to revisit painful experiences and emotions. Two veterans asked not to be identified. Some organizations, as well as some veterans, that I contacted did not respond, and a few declined to be interviewed for personal reasons. One veteran who was eager to share his story was, sadly, unable to do so because he wrestled with his ongoing PTSD issues.

None of the veterans wanted to be portrayed as victims. Without exception, all of them were open, candid, and eager to talk about the impenetrable bond of trust they share with their dogs. They shared their amazement over their dogs' abilities, be they innate or trained. These are deep, loving, and honest human–canine partnerships—relationships forged on mutual dependence and trust.

In sharing these stories, I endeavored to remain true to what the veterans had told me while paring away as much as possible the horrific encounters that they confronted on a regular basis. These stories paint a picture of our nation's heroes who served during the wars in Vietnam, Iraq, and Afghanistan, as well as in the Gulf War era and even in World War II. Ordinary Americans who accomplished extraordinary feats to protect the liberties we hold dear—and the extraordinary dogs who now serve those heroes by reporting for duty twenty-four hours a day, seven days a week. Dogs who became instant therapists, comforting and watching over those struggling with recurring dreams, panic attacks, crippling migraines, insomnia, fear, agoraphobia, loneliness, and the grief associated with

the loss of fellow soldiers. Dogs who guide the blind, retrieve objects, and open and close doors for the physically disabled. Dogs who interrupt nightmares, respond to seizures, and hit buttons that dial 911.

I was moved beyond words upon hearing these accounts of patriotism, and I am honored to share these stories of human and canine heroism with you. In doing so, I have tried to capture the significance and emotion that each story deserves. These are stories of remarkable men and women who risked everything and would freely and enthusiastically do it again to protect our freedom—honorable men and women who balk at being called heroes. Yet heroes they are, for their brave and unselfish service to our great country. Rather than rest on their laurels—for which no one would fault them—many of these veterans are speaking publicly, educating, and advocating for their fellow wounded warriors as well as fundraising to support the training of future service dogs. They continue to volunteer and serve, neither asking for nor expecting anything in return.

If you are looking for a hero—look no further than our military. We can never thank these men and women enough for their sacrifices. My sincerest hope is that readers will recognize and honor our wounded veterans who gave up so much to protect our freedom, as well as the exceptional canines who serve them with such love and devotion.

Author's Note

Before you start reading, there are a few things that I'd like to explain.

When I was writing this book, the veterans were beyond helpful about explaining and clarifying the importance of titles and terminology; for example, "wounded warrior" refers to a veteran injured post-9/11. "Soldier" refers to someone who served in the United States Army, and a Marine is always a Marine, with a capital "M."

You may note that sometimes "Marine" is written as "marine," with a lowercase "m," which I've learned can be insulting to Marines. The Chicago Manual of Style, which is a bible for many book writers, editors, and publishers, does not capitalize military names when they stand alone. For this reason, you may see "Marine" or "marine," depending on its context. It should not be viewed as disrespectful but rather as a standardized literary/editorial style. Similarly, you may see the term "wounded warrior" or "soldier" used more broadly when referring to all veterans, regardless of the military conflict or branch of service.

Unless I am referencing a specific person, when writing of "veterans" or "soldiers" in a general context, I employ "he" or "his." Again, this is done for consistency's sake and simplicity and should not be viewed as disrespectful to the significant number of women serving in our armed forces.

Finally, in this book, dogs are referred to as "he," "she," or "who" rather than as "it" or "that." When speaking generically or when the gender of a dog is unknown, the pronoun "he" is used for simplicity. Again, this is done for consistency's sake and because dogs are much more than an "it."

1

PTSD, TBI, AND MST

PTSD, TBI, AND MST

Making life-and-death decisions, sometimes as often as hourly or with split-second timing, is what many of the 2.7 million Americans deployed to Iraq and Afghanistan do daily. Every decision is a calculation, a potential reward for the risks they took. As one combat veteran said, "You're fighting for your life over there."

Prior to September 11, 2001, most Americans had never heard of Al Qaeda—a fundamentalist Islamic terror network hosted by the Taliban government in Afghanistan. Nearly 3,000 Americans were killed when terrorists hijacked planes and flew them into the World Trade Center, the Pentagon, and a field near Shanksville, Pennsylvania. Almost immediately, the US Armed Forces led the way in beginning a new type of war: a war on terrorism. In response to the attacks, the United States, under President George W. Bush, began combat operations in Afghanistan, officially referred to as Operation Enduring Freedom (OEF), on October 7, 2001.

Separately, because of the belief that Iraq had weapons of mass destruction (WMDs), the war known as Operation Iraqi Freedom (OIF) began on March 19, 2003, with President Bush authorizing the mission to rid Iraq of Saddam Hussein and eliminate his ability to develop WMDs.

Most incredibly, plenty of American soldiers deployed to Iraq and Afghanistan were teenagers on that horrific

September day. Today, those teenagers have grown into some of the finest all-volunteer military fighting forces in the world, having served—and continuing to serve—our country. In the process, a good percentage of them have sustained life-altering injuries.

More so than any other generation of military warriors, advances in body armor, weaponry, strategy, technology, transportation, and battlefield medicine have given troops a better chance of coming home. Today, for the first time in American history, large percentages of injured soldiers returning from the battlefield survive their injuries. Consider, for example, that, according to the National WWII Museum, 416,800 military men were killed during that war. According to the National Archives, more than 3 million American military service members deployed to Vietnam between 1964 and 1975, with more than 58,000 deaths. Figures for 2013 indicate that nearly 4,500 Americans have been killed in Iraq. Add in the Afghanistan war, and the tally jumps to more than 6,600, states an article on McClatchyDC.com. As of September 2012, more than 1.6 million military members

Dogs are loyal to the veterans they serve.

who had been deployed in those two wars had transitioned to veteran status.

Unlike past wars, which were characterized by infectious diseases and catastrophic gunshot wounds, the signature injuries of the wars in Iraq and Afghanistan are emotional trauma resulting in post-traumatic stress disorder (PTSD) and blast-related wounds from improvised explosive devices (IEDs).

The US Department of Defense estimates that, between 2001 and 2014, some 310,000 soldiers were identified as suffering from traumatic brain injury (TBIs), with blasts from IEDs being the most common cause of wounded-in-action injuries and death. History tells us that TBIs are likely as old as warfare, yet the high rate of TBIs in the Iraq and Afghanistan wars has brought increased attention to the effects of blast and penetration (bullets, metal fragments) on the brain.

The wounds of war are not always visible.

Dr. Carolyn Caldwell, a neuropsychologist assigned to Kirk US Army Health Clinic in Maryland, tells the *Fort Hood Sentinel* that the nerves or neurons in our brains can be compared to Silly Putty, and, when stretched too far, the normal chemical activity of the brain is disrupted. The neurons are very elastic, but they can break.

Despite the prevalence of TBIs, there appears to be no secure means of diagnosis and no known ways to prevent or cure them. While the mechanisms of blast-force damage to the brain remain a bit of a mystery, experts theorize that it likely arises from a combination of primary and secondary effects.

The primary effect derives from the blast pressure wave—a spherical wall of gas and air moving faster than the speed of sound that expands until the pressure falls below atmospheric pressure. So intense is it that the blast can easily lift and send a 15-ton armored vehicle into the air, slamming it against rocks, walls, or dusty roadsides. This primary blast wave passes through body armor and bone and is able to disrupt underlying tissues through embedded shear and stress waves. Organ systems with high air content, such as the lungs, stomach, and ears, are highly susceptible, but overpressure can cause damage to the central nervous system as well.

Tertiary blast injury involves acceleration and deceleration forces, such as when a body is propelled and crashes into a fixed structure or the ground. During this type of blast, supersonic wind fragments and hurls objects, creating flying, weaponized projectiles.

A variety of symptoms are associated with a mild TBI (mTBI), or concussion, in which there is minimal or no loss of consciousness; these symptoms include headaches, seizures, motor disorders, sleep disorders, dizziness, visual disturbances, ringing in the ears, mood changes, and cognitive, memory, or speech difficulties. Many of these symptoms overlap those of other problems faced by returning veterans, including PTSD. While many experts object to the "mild" qualifier, many mTBIs are less obvious than the more severe acute TBIs and therefore may be missed or overlooked. The one-year estimated cost associated with treating mild to moderate TBIs is between $591 million and $910 million.

A 2008 study published by the RAND Corporation notes that approximately 20 percent of the 1.6 million military personnel who had deployed to the wars in Iraq and Afghanistan—roughly

During WWII, 416,800 members of the US military lost their lives.

300,000—reported symptoms of PTSD, stress disorder, or major depression (yet only slightly more than half have sought treatment). The Department of Veterans Affairs' National Center for PTSD estimates that the number is between 11 and 20 percent, whereas a 2015 report published in the *Journal of Anxiety Disorder*, which analyzed thirty-three PTSD studies published between 2007 and 2013, estimates the prevalence at 23 percent. Research suggests that the number climbs even higher when combined with a TBI.

Furthermore, the 2008 study estimates that PTSD and depression among returning service members will cost the nation as much as $62 billion in the two years following deployment—an amount that includes both direct medical care and costs related to lost productivity and suicide. The report adds that investing in high-quality treatment could save close to $2 billion within two years.

Although PTSD wasn't formally recognized as a mental health issue attributed to war conditions until about 1980, a 2015 article by Adam Magers titled "New Evidence of PTSD in 1300 BC: What We Can Learn from History" tells us of emotional trauma during the Assyrian Dynasty in 1300 BC. In "Suffering in Silence: Psychological Disorders and Soldiers in the American Civil War," published in the April 2013 *Armstrong Undergraduate Journal of History*, Sarah A. M. Ford recalls Greek historian Herodotus, who wrote in 480 BC of a Spartan soldier who was "taken off the front lines due to his trembling and later took his own life in shame."

Evidence of war-related emotional trauma dates back to the Civil War and even earlier.

More recently, diaries and letters from the American Civil War suggest that soldiers at that time also struggled with psychological disorders, or what was known as "soldier's heart" during the mid- and late nineteenth century. Stories abound of World War I soldiers suffering from "shell shock," a term believed to have derived from the concussion-producing impact of the shells, which disrupted the physiology of the brain. Nostalgia, *heimweh* (homesickness), *maladie du pays*, and *estar roto* ("to be broken") are a few of PTSD's other earlier names.

Gradually, psychiatrists began to realize that the injuries were emotional as opposed to physiological. Sadly, however, mental health experts at that time continued to believe that PTSD surfaced primarily in men who were "weak in character."

World War II brought us the terms "combat neurosis," which gave way to "combat exhaustion" and "battle fatigue." Only after the Vietnam War did the term PTSD begin to enter America's lexicon. Yet, as history reminds us, the terminology is really just a new name for an old story. PTSD (and the accompanying suicide epidemic) is possibly the most misunderstood condition affecting veterans. Experts say that determining the suicide rate among veterans with any accuracy is difficult, yet the Veterans Administration (VA) estimates that a veteran dies by suicide every 65 minutes. Defined by the American Psychiatric Association, PTSD is "an anxiety (emotional) disorder which stems from a particular incident evoking significant stress." The most prevalent conditions for veterans include combat events—particularly witnessing someone being injured or killed or seeing or handling dead bodies—although studies indicate that soldiers need not experience combat to suffer from PTSD.

The term "PTSD" did not come into use until after the Vietnam War.

Typical PTSD symptoms include depression, anxiety, stress, hypervigilance, exaggerated startle response, nightmares, night tremors or recurring dreams about war, flashbacks, memory loss, difficulty concentrating, and isolation, to name a few. These symptoms all too often generate a tendency for the affected to seek relief in alcohol, drugs, or suicide.

MST

Military sexual trauma (MST)—a form of sexual assault ranging from unwanted sexual conduct to rape that occurs in the military—is a stress disorder related to but not as widely known as PTSD. Despite the federal government's zero-tolerance policy, sexual assault in the military continues to rise. The Department of Defense's Annual Report on Sexual Assault in the Military found for fiscal year 2014 an 11 percent increase over 2013 numbers. Out of 6,120 reports of sexual assault in 2014, there were 4,768 service member victims who made reports for incidents that occurred during military service. It's not clear whether the increase is attributable to an increased number of assaults, increased reporting, or both.

Long conflicts with multiple deployments have taken a widespread emotional toll on military personnel. According to a report published by the National Institutes of Health, by the end of 2010, nearly 2.2 million service members had deployed to Iraq and Afghanistan. Of those deployed, 57 percent deployed only once and 43 percent deployed multiple times. Of those who deployed more than once, nearly two-thirds deployed twice, while one-quarter deployed three times, and about 15 percent deployed four or more times.

Those familiar with PTSD note that it can be "triggered" by any sight, smell, or event that prompts a memory of the trauma to come crashing in. Sounds that resemble gunfire, such as the seemingly innocuous sound of a can of peas falling off a shelf in a grocery store or two shopping carts banging together, can trigger memories of distress. For many veterans, the simple act of driving—especially passing under bridges or overpasses—can cause memories of the battlefield to surface, as can the seemingly innocent sight of trash on the side of the road (Iraqis used it to conceal explosives) or the sound of children crying.

That's where a specially trained service dog comes in. Unlike a therapist, a service dog is by the veteran's side twenty-four hours a day, seven days a week, helping him or her navigate life's daily stressors, reducing stress and anxiety, and providing companionship and affection.

Many, but not all, PTSD-trained dogs are taught to *block* or *watch*, behaviors that are aimed at keeping strangers from coming too close, and this enables many veterans to feel more comfortable about venturing into public. Yet, according to the Department of Veterans Affairs National Center for PTSD, veterans who use service dogs do not have the chance to learn if they can handle stressful situations without their dogs. According to the VA website, "Although people with PTSD who have a service dog for a physical disability or emotional-support dog may feel comforted by the animal, there is some chance they may continue to believe they cannot do certain things on their own.

Becoming dependent on the dog can get in the way of the recovery process for PTSD."

Many of the veterans profiled in this book disagree, with nearly all of them teetering on the brink of suicide before their service dogs changed their lives by helping them leave the battlefield behind as they reintegrated back into society. Interest in the use of service dogs in treating PTSD has increased dramatically, with many service-dog training organizations noting a six-month to two-year waiting list. It's also one of the reasons that the federal government—not known for being at the forefront of alternative therapies/medical treatments—is spending millions of dollars to study whether scientific research supports anecdotal reports that dogs might speed up recovery from the psychological wounds of war. (Currently, the VA provides benefits to support the use of service dogs only for visual, hearing, or mobility impairments.) However, a countless number of veterans will tell you that they don't need a study to provide evidence and that they are living proof that specially trained service dogs can change lives for the better and, in many instances, even save lives.

Jake Young and Marshall Peters of Warrior Canine Connection with mobility-dog-in-training Lundy.

BRIAN ANDERSON
&
HERO

*It is the soldier, not the reporter, who has given us
freedom of the press.*
*It is the soldier, not the poet, who has given us
freedom of speech.*
*It is the soldier, not the campus organizer, who has
given us the freedom to demonstrate.*
*It is the soldier, who salutes the flag, who serves
beneath the flag,*
*And whose coffin is draped by the flag, who allows
the protestor to burn the flag.*

~ Excerpted from a quote by Charles M. Province

Hero gently licks Brian Anderson's cheek, interrupting his dream. It's a recurring dream that puts Anderson back on the battlefield in Afghanistan—a chaotic, intense combat zone where Anderson, amid all of the carnage, is fighting for his life. Gradually, an overwhelming sense of calmness washes over him as he feels Hero's head resting gently against his cheek. Anderson lies still, eyes closed, the battlefield drifting farther away in his dream. Hero's touch softens.

"When I woke up," explains Anderson, "I realized that it wasn't Hero's head on my cheek; it was his paw. He was standing over me, watching me calm down. I remember thinking, 'How loving. This is a beautiful thing.'" These were feelings he had not felt since before the war.

Brian remains a devoted patriot, committed to helping others who have served the United States.

This was a pivotal point in the human–canine relationship for Anderson, a retired Green Beret who joined the military shortly after 9/11 and spent ten years in the United States Army—first as a photojournalist and then as a Green Beret, 2nd Battalion, 7th Special Forces Group (Airborne), with multiple deployments in direct combat. Anderson, the recipient of three Bronze Stars, one with valor, has zero hesitation when it comes to sharing his touching story about Hero, his aptly named service dog. But that wasn't always the case.

At first, Anderson—"the big, bad barrel-chested freedom fighter"—a guardian of freedom, balked at the notion of a service dog and the descriptors that he felt accompanied one. As one of 6,500 elite special-forces-qualified soldiers who are some of the most highly skilled men in the military, who overwhelm hostile forces with blistering small-arms fire, engage in close-quarter battles, breach and clear rooms, and jump out of airplanes at 30,000 feet, Anderson's struggle was internal. He needed and wanted a service dog, but he

Brian with one of the Afghan locals that his team had been deployed to help.

Brian with best friend, Sgt. 1st Class Calvin Harrison, who was killed during their Afghanistan deployment.

did not welcome the attention that was likely to accompany a dog wearing a service vest. *Here's Brian Anderson and his service dog. Here's Brian Anderson, veteran. He needs a service dog.*

Firebase Cobra, a small, remote American military support base located in central Afghanistan's Uruzgan Province, roughly 100 miles north of Kandahar and 7,800 miles from Anderson's current home in Florida, is one of the most violent and dangerous areas of Afghanistan. As one expert puts it, it's a place where soldiers are all but guaranteed to confront the enemy every time they step outside the wire.

September 29, 2010—Members of the elite special-forces team, including Anderson and his best friend, Sgt. 1st Class Calvin Harrison, a Green Beret medical sergeant, set out on their mission of clearing ramshackle villages—villages that no one outside of Afghanistan has ever heard of—of Taliban insurgents who intimidate villagers and try to kill US forces with sniper fire and IEDs. "We went into the villages in Afghanistan. We worked with their communities," explains Anderson. "Our job was to help them help themselves—to help them develop perseverance."

An eight-hour firefight ended in the death of Harrison and Senior Airman Mark Forester, a US Air Force combat controller, and left Anderson with visions that would haunt him for years. Nothing in Anderson's intimidating physical appearance identified him as injured or disabled, yet the hidden psychological wounds that came from multiple deployments in direct combat began to take a toll.

Anderson was told that he suffered from PTSD in 2012, after returning to civilian life. Prior to being matched with Hero, he struggled with stress, anxiety, anger, and the recurring images that come from killing men and seeing fellow soldiers killed. Despite burying the images, seemingly innocuous behavior, such as a child whining, could send him into a full-blown panic attack.

Brain-imaging studies have shown that veterans living with PTSD are more distractible—both by neutral stimuli and by those that remind them of the trauma they suffered, reports Kim Puchir in an article titled "The Role of Service Animals in Recovery" for the *National Alliance on Mental Illness.* "I'd wash dishes and imagine a bullet going through my head," says Anderson. "I would drive down the road and look at the car next to me, and one of my best friends, Calvin, who was killed on one of our missions in Afghanistan, he'd be driving the car next to me. I thought they were blood-pressure issues, diabetes, or something like that," says Anderson. "When I went in to be checked out, they said, 'No, you're having panic attacks. This is post-traumatic stress.'"

Like many soldiers, Anderson was struggling with the fallout from the sights, sounds, and smells of war. Anderson knew that something was going to happen. Something always happened. But it was the uncertainty of never knowing when or where the next sniper or ambush would hit or the next IED might go off. Despite the demanding and dangerous duty, Anderson remains proud of his service. Fighting for freedom is why he joined the military. Why he became a Green Beret.

When Anderson returned stateside, a VA psychiatrist prescribed three medications. His primary-care physician prescribed three more medications. None of them worked. A standard course of PTSD treatment, according to the VA's National Center for PTSD, is known as prolonged exposure therapy—the retelling of traumatic memories over and over again as a means of desensitizing soldiers. It worked with Anderson for a while, but his PTSD symptoms, such as hypervigilance, continued, often outrunning him. Before Hero, Anderson couldn't sleep. He wanted to sleep—needed to sleep—but a component of PTSD is the inability to sleep. Well-meaning friends and family members told him to lock it up, box it up, and let it go.

Anderson recalls the first day that he met Hero, the specially trained PTSD service dog who would heal his soul and change his life. It was October 27, 2014. "It was an instant bond," says Anderson. "He walked up and sat down next to me. We bonded immediately." They've been together ever since.

Hero, a purebred Golden Retriever bred by Traci Thompson of Country Goldens in Graysville, Tennessee, and donated

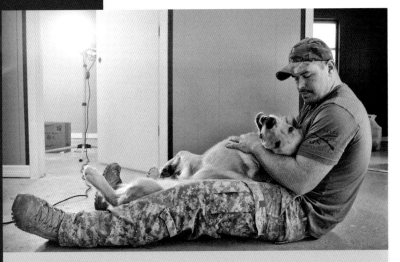

Brian and Hero are completely at ease with one another.

Hero is Brian's ever-attentive constant companion.

Just petting Hero can lessen any stress or anxiety that Brian may feel.

Hero is ready to help in whatever way he is needed!

to Patriot Service Dogs, Inc., a Tennessee-based 501(c)(3) nonprofit, personifies the breed's quiet, intelligent, responsive temperament and love of life. These are among the characteristics that have kept the Golden Retriever ranked as one of America's favorite breeds for decades. The Golden's first-rate ability to comfort and provide physical and emotional support to the injured and lonely make it an ultimate service- and therapy-dog breed.

Hero was matched with Anderson and donated to him through Patriot Service Dogs, Inc., after he completed puppy socialization and advanced training through a prison puppy program at the Lowell Women's Prison in Ocala, Florida, where inmates train the dogs until they are between eighteen months and two years old. "We strive to make a difference in the lives of those who have given so much to our freedom," says Julie Drexel, president and co-founder of Patriot Service Dogs, Inc.

Anderson still has anxious moments because of PTSD, explaining how symptoms can go from 0 to 60 miles per hour in a nanosecond. The seemingly simple task of driving from point A to point B can trigger hypervigilance, anxiety, and stress and cause images of the battlefield to come crashing in.

"I hate being boxed in," says Anderson. "As soldiers, we're trained not to get boxed in, to overcome obstacles. When driving, I feel boxed in, so I'm always looking for . . . an escape route." Sensing his owner's increased stress and anxiety, Hero climbs into the front seat and lays his head on Anderson's lap, essentially calming him, lowering his anxiety, and bringing him back to the present.

In very much the same way, Hero is trained to help Anderson navigate chaotic, noisy, crowded places, such as grocery stores, restaurants, baseball or football stadiums, and even Disney World. So strong is their relationship and so adept is Hero at scrutinizing Anderson's emotions, monitoring his breathing and pulse, and detecting shifts in his body language that Hero frequently alerts to Anderson even before Anderson's anxiety and stress build up to explosive levels.

Like many veterans returning from deployment, Anderson also experienced feelings of detachment and had problems forming relationships. "In the military, you're with your peers and battle buddies 24/7. You go from having people around 24/7 to being isolated. Your family and friends don't understand what you went through. They want to help, and they try to help, but they don't understand. Dogs don't ask questions. They're just there. Some things on the battlefield might be done out of fear or anger, but you're fighting for your life over there. With Hero, there's no debating. I don't have to second-guess myself or prove myself right or wrong or explain myself. He's just there. Always there. He's 100-percent loyal."

What Hero does for Anderson emotionally and spiritually may be difficult for many people to understand—especially those who have never shared or experienced the strong bond that only an animal can provide—and that's OK with Anderson. Every conversation with Anderson comes back to what he, as well as others, can do and are doing to improve the lives of wounded veterans. "I was called to service not by a draft but by my own personal convictions," says Anderson. Returning to civilian life, Anderson felt he was called to service once again—this time, back in the United States as an advocate for wounded veterans.

That portion of Anderson's life began in 2013, when the prolonged exposure

Visitors to the Veterans Alternative Therapy Center get some complimentary canine therapy, courtesy of Hero.

therapy recommended by the VA didn't work, and Anderson turned to accelerated resolution therapy (ART)—a seemingly unconventional yet effective treatment for combat-related symptoms of PTSD that came on the scene in 2007. Why it works remains a bit of a mystery.

"No one left behind" is the slogan and the aim of the Pasco County Stand Down event.

Studies at the University of South Florida College of Nursing Research Center and published in the *Behavioral Sciences* journal indicate that the two-phase treatment—a combination of evidence-based psychotherapies and the use of eye movements—alleviates psychological trauma symptoms and related disorders such as depression and anxiety. In the simplest of terms, the patient reimagines a prior traumatic experience, and the physical and psychological sensations that occur with that recollection are lessened using a series of left-to-right eye movements in sets of forty. Simply put, it changes how the brain remembers images.

"After one treatment, the therapy took the bad memories that constantly resurfaced and put them in the proper order or long-term storage," says Anderson.

With Hero by his side, Anderson is on a mission to educate wounded veterans, and people in general, about ART, as well as about the benefits of service dogs and what can happen when they are paired with veterans. In November 2014, Anderson teamed up with business partner and US Air Force veteran Janel Norton to open the first Veterans Alternative Therapy Center in Holiday, Florida, to provide veterans with restorative therapies, including ART and yoga. Additionally, in the not-too-distant future, Anderson and Norton hope to add a program that trains veterans to train service dogs.

"Our veterans served us, and now we must serve them," says Anderson. "We cannot allow our returning veterans to become statistics like our warriors before them; rather, as a community, we must find that personal conviction within us to serve our men and woman as they return to civilian population."

Anderson has experienced firsthand that Hero is much more than a service dog. He's with Anderson 24/7 and has also become the official "unofficial" greeter to veterans coming to the Veterans Alternative Therapy Center who are filled with doubt, hesitation, anxiety, and stress. Hero helps break the ice, according to Anderson, who recounts a recent late-night meeting with an anxious, stressed veteran teetering on the edge. Hero climbed onto the couch and became a lap dog to the veteran, who immediately connected with the dog by petting and stroking him. By easing the veteran's anxiety, the man was able to talk, reach out, ask for help, and hopefully take a step toward a brighter future.

Some veterans come to the center just to see Hero, to hang out with him, to pet him. Others bring their own dogs to play with this Golden Retriever, who has an innate love of life. Simply watching the dogs run and play together is proving therapeutic for many veterans struggling with PTSD.

Additionally, Anderson started the current version of the Pasco County Stand Down, a community-wide event that provides homeless and at-risk veterans with a broad range of highly needed services. Attendees find Hero by Anderson's side throughout the three-day event, providing unconditional love and support to not only Anderson but also to other veterans.

Unlike a therapist, Hero is always with Anderson—by his side twenty-four hours a day, seven days a week. He rides in the car with Anderson. He curls up under the table at restaurants while Anderson eats, and he quietly sleeps under Anderson's desk while he's working. He accompanies Anderson to the store, to business meetings, to fundraisers, and to dinners—including a dinner with Florida's governor, Rick Scott. "Hero is 100-percent loyal. I depend on him and vice versa," says Anderson. "He connects me to an emotional place."

Wherever you find Brian, you'll find Hero nearby.

JASON
&
BUCKLES

*You gain strength, courage, and confidence by
every experience in which you really stop to look
fear in the face. You must do the thing which you
think you cannot.*

~ Eleanor Roosevelt

Attached to the Marine Corps Special Forces Unit, Jason* deployed with nine combat
operations in support of the wars in Afghanistan and Iraq, although not all of the
deployments were full deployments. An IED ended his military service—a split
second in time that forever changed his life. After leaving the military in 2003, Jason
continues to struggle with the physical injuries that have left him with multiple organ
damage, severe nerve damage in his back and legs, and PTSD.

* Jason's name has been changed and last name withheld to protect his privacy.

Jason and Buckles became a pair following training with Veterans Moving Forward.

Following in the footsteps of his father and grandfather, who also served, Jason doesn't regret his time in service. Despite all of the physical and mental pain he experiences daily, he would gladly go back and serve again if he could. Once a Marine, always a Marine, and, like a true Marine, Jason is moving forward with the help of a specially trained service dog. Buckles, a two-year-old yellow Labrador Retriever named after Corporal Frank R. Buckles, who lived to be 110 years old and was designated the last living American World War I veteran, helps Jason with daily tasks that he is no longer able to do himself.

Calm, intelligent, and friendly, Buckles, along with his litter brother, Jug (see page 110), was purchased from a northern Virginia breeder and trained by Veterans Moving Forward (VMF), a 501 (c)(3) nonprofit organization with the goal of helping veterans move forward with their lives. Once Buckles completed his training, VMF donated him to Jason.

Buckles is alert and attentive to Jason's needs.

Jason and Buckles had an immediate connection that grew into an exceptional bond.

Like many veterans struggling with the fallout from combat, Jason isolated himself from family and friends. He lives with the invisible wounds of PTSD, including flashbacks and nightmares, and he struggles with nerve damage that causes numbness and shooting pain in his back and legs, which affect his mobility and balance. He's unsteady on his feet, and navigating stairs and uneven surfaces is painfully difficult.

While attending PTSD recovery classes through the VA, Jason met several fellow service members with service dogs—something he had not considered. He researched organizations online and found that a specially trained dog could help him with mobility issues and be his assistant in everyday tasks that able-bodied people take for granted, such as walking, taking laundry out of the washer and putting it in the dryer, or even bending down to retrieve a shoe or dropped cell phone. Buckles helps Jason with all of that—and more.

Jason applied to several organizations but was drawn to VMF. "I never thought I would get in," says Jason. After a lengthy application process, Jason underwent a three-hour interview with the veteran–canine selection committee at VMF and eventually met some dogs in a public setting. "I liked Buckles right away. I connected with him, but I wanted the trainer's opinion, too. I wanted to make sure I was picking the best dog for me."

True to the Labrador Retriever breed, Buckles is eager and willing to learn, work, and retrieve, which made him an ideal service-dog candidate. "He is very aware of his surroundings and extremely adaptable," says trainer Betsy Khol Abdeen. "During his formal training, Buckles worked with a lot of different trainers, so he was able to transition quickly to being Jason's service dog."

Buckles is trained to know when Jason needs a break.

Buckles has been Jason's constant companion since March 2015. Once the pair was matched with each other, Buckles, who already had a solid foundation of basic obedience skills and service-dog training, underwent customized training specific to Jason's needs. "He is trained to retrieve my medications on command, which includes opening the drawer where they are kept and bringing the bag to me," says Jason, "and he's trained to remind me to take them."

Buckles's training also includes helping Jason with balance and mobility, including walking and going up and down stairs. Trained to stop every so often while on stairs, Buckles regularly checks to make sure that Jason is OK until the two of them have made their way safely up or down. "I'm 6'3" and 255 pounds," says Jason, "I use him to help brace me, but not brace my entire weight."

In addition to helping with equilibrium issues and everyday tasks, Buckles is trained to help keep Jason calm while in public. Every veteran has individual anxiety markers, such as hand wringing, knee bouncing, or other self-calming gestures. VMF trains their dogs to recognize their individual veterans' signature anxiety markers. When Buckles sees Jason displaying these behaviors, he will do something to interrupt Jason—whether it's a nudge or a paw or a bark—to break the cycle, stop the escalation of anxiety or panic, and let Jason know, "Hey, we need to get out of here."

Jason and Buckles continue to train weekly with Abdeen to fortify Buckles' skills both at Jason's home and in public settings. Certainly not a novice when it comes to dogs, Jason has worked with law-enforcement dogs, and a portion of his military service included working as a handler with military dogs trained to guard detainees.

"The purpose and reward and training between military dogs and service dogs are completely different," says Jason.

Their first week together, Buckles tested his boundaries—wanting to know how much he could get away with. "He's a service dog," says Jason, "but he's still a dog." However, each day, their bond grows stronger. Buckles now understands Jason's routine and how he wants to do things. When Buckles' isn't working, he can be

found jumping into Jason's lap, sitting on the couch next to him, cuddling, or playing.

Life has changed considerably for Jason since being matched with Buckles, who goes everywhere Jason goes. With Buckles by his side, Jason is less reclusive and more comfortable and confident venturing out into public and going on family outings and get-togethers. He sleeps better at night, too, because Buckles provides a sense of security. "He helps me to get along better," says Jason. "I'm not on as many medications, and I'm better able to help my wife and help with our firstborn child."

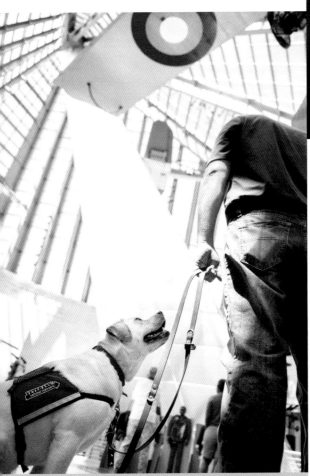

Jason can handle public outings and enjoy more of life with Buckles by his side.

2

PRISON PUPPY PROGRAMS

PRISON PUPPY PROGRAMS

After losing both legs to a landmine in Afghanistan, a retired veteran received a two-year-old Labrador Retriever through the Assistance Dogs for Veterans (formerly Canines for Combat Veterans) program. The program is run by the National Education for Assistance Dogs Services (NEADS), and, most remarkably, the service dog was trained by a prison inmate in the organization's Prison Pup Partnership program.

The idea of having prison inmates socialize and train service dogs for veterans may seem disconcerting, considering that training dogs is no easy feat. Granted, it's not rocket science, but some of the behaviors are relatively complex. After all, owners pay professional trainers hundreds, if not thousands, of dollars to train their dogs to come, sit, lie down, stay, and go potty in the appropriate place. Still, millions of dogs end up in shelters each year for displaying behavioral problems and breaking rules they didn't even know existed.

So what qualifies a prison inmate to train a dog for organizations that pride themselves on having the highest standards of training? "Prison inmates are carefully screened—twice—and they must be good, qualified

handlers," says John Moon, Director of Client Programs and Community Engagement at NEADS. A prison liaison screens and selects appropriate inmate handlers who have applied to be puppy trainers, and then a NEADS trainer conducts additional interviews. "Inmates have very structured environments. Their movements are monitored, [and] they have specific times for breakfast, lunch, and dinner." And, of course, they're not going anywhere, so they have plenty of time on their hands.

Inmates at ten New England prisons train 90 to 95 percent of the assistance dogs for NEADS, with one inmate and one dog per cell. (A backup inmate participates in case the primary handler is unable to complete the program.) NEADS trainers provide detailed training protocols and instructions. They also make regular weekly visits and support the inmates, who spend most of their time taking the puppies on scheduled potty breaks and socializing them in the recreation areas, dining halls, visiting rooms, and other common areas to expose them to different people and the different sights and sounds they're likely to encounter as adult dogs.

NEADS trainers teach the inmate handlers how to perform everyday dog-care duties.

The handlers also introduce the puppies to basic obedience commands, including *come*, *sit*, *down*, and *stay.* If any problems arise, the NEADS trainers will help the handlers deal with them.

Inmate handlers also learn how to provide basic first aid, monitor canine health, and groom the dogs, which helps accustom the puppies to handling, brushing, nail clipping, and other routine tasks.

To maximize the puppies' full range of socialization experiences, they stay at the prison during the week and go home with specially trained "weekend puppy raisers" on Friday nights. The puppy raisers take the puppies around town for additional socialization and exposure to typical life experiences that are difficult to replicate in a prison setting. Each Sunday night, the puppies go back to prison to start another week of training. This process unfolds for

Graham is a NEADS service dog in training.

about fourteen to eighteen months, after which the puppies are "released" from prison and returned to NEADS for placement with veterans.

NEADS's Prison Pup Partnership started in 1998, and today the ten New England correctional facilities typically house six to eight dogs (up to as many as twelve dogs, in some instances) each. Roughly ninety dogs enter the NEADS Prison Pup Partnership yearly, and the program has roughly a 50-percent success rate.

A NEADS prison-trained service dog helps with the grocery shopping.

Dogs wash out of the program for any number of reasons, including environmental fear, such as a fear of shadows or novel objects. Moon adopted one dog who loved carrying sticks everywhere but didn't make it through the program because if you stood the stick up in front of him, he became terrified. Despite the trainers' best efforts, they were unable to desensitize his fear of vertical sticks—and a "vertical stick" could easily translate into a broom or rake or walking cane leaning up against a wall in a veteran's home or workplace. Today, "stick dog" is Moon's cherished companion.

NEADS isn't the only service-dog organization that utilizes prison programs. The practice of prison training programs has grown phenomenally. One of the earliest modern-day canine prison programs can be traced to the Purdy Treatment Center for Women in Gig Harbor, Washington. The 1981 program taught female inmates to train and groom dogs from a local animal shelter. As a result, the dogs became more adoptable and were saved from euthanasia.

John J. Ensminger writes in his book *Service and Therapy Dogs in American Society* that at least thirty-six states have some sort of prison animal program. "Historically, prisons often had farms, and programs involving the care of animals have not been uncommon in minimum-security facilities, but dog-training programs began to be developed mostly after 2000. There are now at least 150 such programs."

Kent Phyfe's new service dog, Mike (see page 55), was raised by an inmate through America's VetDogs' (AVD) Prison Puppy Program. Five state correctional institutions in Massachusetts, four in Maryland, one in Connecticut, and one soon to open in Florida are home to AVD prison puppies. Similar to other programs, inmates raise and train puppies who will one day work as service dogs for wounded veterans. The puppies live in their handlers' cells, and the handlers work with them on house-training, crate training, and basic puppy commands. Following instruction and guidance from AVD trainers, inmates also teach service-dog tasks, such as retrieving dropped items, tugging doors open, pushing handicapped-door buttons, and providing brace and balance on stairs. Statistics have shown that prison-raised dogs are usually so skilled that they are able to go through the final training process in half the normal time of home-raised dogs.

Phyfe has a unique perspective because he has been involved with AVD's prison program at Enfield Correctional Institution in Enfield, Connecticut, since its inception. He has also had two service dogs—Iris, a Lab mix rescued from a shelter, who was trained outside the prison program, and, more recently, Mike, a purebred Labrador Retriever who, as mentioned, was raised and trained by an inmate. Granted, Iris's and Mike's breeding and history are worlds apart, but Phyfe could not be happier with the advanced abilities of his inmate-trained service dog.

A prison-raised dog also has special meaning for Phyfe. "To have been involved with the VetDogs prison program and see how it helps change communities and prisoners is icing on the cake for me," says Phyfe.

Many of the inmate handlers meet and get to know the veterans for whom they are training dogs. Brian Anderson, whose service dog Hero (see page 26) came out of Patriot Service Dogs' prison program at Lowell Women's Prison in Ocala, Florida, has plans to start a program that teaches veterans to train service dogs through his newly founded Veterans Alternative Therapy Center in Holiday, Florida. He hopes to hire Hero's inmate handler when she's released from prison.

Except for the standard-issue prison garb, many of the female inmates would not appear out of place at any shopping mall or doctor's office. They range in age, and many of

A Yellow Lab practices using a rope to tug a door open.

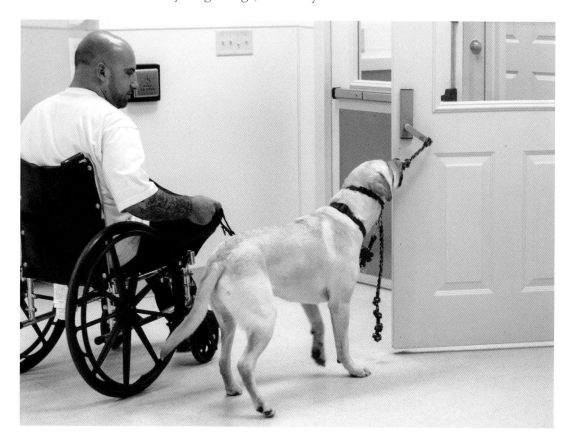

Service dogs are taught to open refrigerator doors and retrieve items from inside.

them are mothers. Some prison-animal programs exclude certain prisoners based on the nature of their convictions, but others do not. In most prisons, inmates with a history of abuse toward humans or animals are automatically excluded. "We're not opposed to considering an inmate doing a life sentence," says Moon, "as long as that inmate is a good and qualified handler."

Ironically, these inmates who have lost their freedom are training dogs for wounded veterans who have fought for freedom. Touching to everyone is the fact that these dogs don't care about the difference between a prisoner and a veteran. They don't know and they don't care whether the person is wearing prison garb, camouflage, or military dress blues. Dogs respond to kindness, patience, repetition, and consistency. These inmates love what they are doing, and it's reflected in how they train the dogs.

In the process of training dogs to complete tasks that injured veterans can never take for granted, such as turning on and off a light, opening and closing a door, retrieving a dropped item, or even going out in public or sleeping without the anxiety of recurring flashbacks or nightmares, the inmates have learned a lot about themselves and, in the process, have become better people as well.

KENT PHYFE & IRIS

Rangers, lead the way!

~ Brigadier General Norman D. Cota, Assistant Division
Commander of the 29th Infantry Division

On the job only five days, a mixed-breed rescue named Iris helped save Kent Phyfe's life. Phyfe's brain transmitted crazy signals to his heart, sending it into arrhythmia, a life-threatening condition for the Army veteran. By licking Phyfe's face, Iris was able to wake him so he could hit the "call doctor" button.

"The rescued has become the rescuer," says Phyfe. "She is an absolutely amazing dog. She does everything I've asked her to do. I don't know where I'd be without her." Without Iris, chances are high that Phyfe wouldn't be around to share his story. Medically retired from the military and deemed 100-percent disabled, he was no longer allowed to work or even drive. Going anywhere meant relying on someone else to drive him. Like many veterans struggling with PTSD and TBI, Phyfe isolated himself at home, fell into a deep depression, and teetered on the brink of suicide.

Joining the US Army at seventeen through their delayed-entry program, Phyfe left for basic training seven days after graduating from high school in 1981. Eventually, he would go on to Ranger school and then the 82nd Airborne Division, continuing his military service

Iris is alert and attentive to Kent and their surroundings.

Iris is proud to wear her America's VetDogs service vest.

with the 1st Special Forces Group (Airborne) and the 10th SFG (A). During his fifteen-year military career, Phyfe served all over the world, averaging about 300 days each year overseas on missions. "I wanted to serve my country, and I wanted the adventure," says Phyfe.

In 1996, while preparing to be promoted from sergeant first class to master sergeant, a routine medical examination discovered that Phyfe's aortic valve was severely damaged. Doctors at Walter Reed Army Medical Center (now Walter Reed National Military Medical Center) replaced the faulty valve with a titanium one, and, shortly thereafter, Phyfe was medically retired. Five years later, doctors discovered that he had an ascending aortic aneurysm and had developed cardiogenic syncope—a medical condition in which communication between the brain and cardiovascular system short-circuits—which causes Phyfe to pass out.

In addition to his cardiac issues, years of combat and airborne missions as an elite special-forces-qualified solider—"the best of the best"—had left Phyfe with back and knee problems.

A Labrador Retriever mix, Iris has shown great trainability and unwavering devotion to Kent.

At his doctor's urging, Phyfe went in search of a service dog, which led him to Iris. The rescued dog not only saved Phyfe's life, she also gave him back his life.

Iris was sprung from a Georgia animal shelter, and, as is the case with many rescues, her history and pedigree were unknown. How and why the 60-pound Labrador Retriever mix ended up alone, confined behind metal gates, remains a mystery, but perhaps her situation was somehow synonymous with Phyfe's, who, through situations beyond his control, had become a prisoner in his own home.

Yet, life seemed to have a plan for this lucky gal, whose Lab ancestors were bred for retrieving instinct, working ability, and temperament— traits that have allowed the breed to adapt to work beyond the shooting field and, more specifically, become supreme service dogs and guide dogs as well as search-and-rescue and substance-detection workers.

Iris was rescued, trained, and donated through America's VetDogs (AVD), a Smithtown, New York, 501(c)(3) nonprofit started by the Guide Dog Foundation for the Blind as a part of a pilot program to train shelter dogs to become service dogs to military veterans living with physical or emotional disabilities. While AVD still has the ability to take in shelter dogs, most of the dogs utilized today are selectively bred and trained by the organization, which evaluates fifty to seventy dogs per year, with roughly 70 percent of the dogs qualifying for service-dog work.

"When I showed up at the America's VetDogs campus, I was terrified," says Phyfe. "This dog I was about to meet could change

Blocking

Many of today's PTSD dogs are trained to "block" by creating a barrier, thereby preventing people from crowding around the veteran. Iris is trained to block by pulling Phyfe away from people when he becomes frazzled in a crowd.

my life. I had seen other brothers that had found something that allowed them to go forward, and now I was going to meet my pup—my hope of moving forward."

When Iris turned her brown eyes on Phyfe, his fear disappeared. Five days later, while still training at the AVD campus, Iris went to work and performed the job that she was trained to do—wake up Phyfe when his heart starts beating abnormally.

Although many heart arrhythmias (irregular heartbeats) are harmless, Phyfe's already weakened heart presents life-threatening symptoms. Trained to recognize when Phyfe's heartbeat goes haywire, Iris will lick Phyfe's face to alert him. If he's awake, he can move in certain ways to get his heart beating normally.

In the event that Phyfe goes into full arrhythmia and passes out, Iris is trained to hit a button that is directly wired to 911. She then barks so that the EMTs can identify Phyfe's house. If Phyfe begins to pass out while in public, Iris will jump on Phyfe's lap to hold him in the chair until help arrives. In either scenario, she stays with Phyfe—licking his face, trying to wake him—until the paramedics arrive, and then she backs off so they can treat him. But her job doesn't end there. She rides to the hospital with Phyfe until the doctors make sure he is OK.

Prior to being matched with Iris, Phyfe had a medical device—similar to a pacemaker—surgically implanted in his chest to alert him when his heart started beating irregularly. So in tune is Iris with Phyfe that she was able to detect a problem at the exact moment that the device picked up the irregular heartbeat. So proficient is she at detecting fluctuations in Phyfe's heartbeat that the device was eventually removed, and today Phyfe relies solely on Iris to detect and alert him to any irregularities or fluctuations in his heartbeat.

With Iris by his side, Kent is able to drive and travel.

"Iris had no problems with electrical storms until we were matched together," says Phyfe. "Now, if there's an electrical storm, she'll lie directly on top of me. If there are others in the house, she'll corral everyone, and then she'll calm down."

A dual-purpose service dog, Iris is also trained to mitigate

Kent Phyfe and Mike meet for the first time

Mike was comfortable with Kent right away, rolling over for some belly rubs the first time they met.

the effects of PTSD. The bond between Phyfe and Iris is so strong that she is able to immediately sense the slightest elevation in Phyfe's anxiety and stress levels. Loud noises, such as fireworks, do not bother Iris; however, they normally trigger stress and anxiety in veterans struggling with PTSD, including Phyfe. When Iris senses his anxiety rising, such as when they're at a baseball game, she will pull him toward the exit and away from the crowds and noises. She will crawl into his lap to calm him and bring him back to the present. She's also trained to interrupt nightmares by jumping on Phyfe.

"We are truly a team that is there for each other—no questions—just like being in a foxhole," Phyfe says. Iris has taken to everyone in the family as well. By taking care of Phyfe, Iris takes care of the entire family. "They feel better leaving me alone," says Phyfe. "Iris has brought so much love into the house. She brought my family back together, stopped me from becoming a statistic, and helped me have a goal in life again."

A loyal companion and the very embodiment of love, Iris shares an exceptional bond with Phyfe in a way that most dog owners may never truly understand. Thanks to Iris, Phyfe has regained his confidence and independence, and, equally importantly, he has not experienced a full-on arrhythmia since being matched with her. His syncope rates are down, and, when they do occur, they are much smaller events. As a result, he has been cleared to drive again, which allows him to pursue his two passions: photography (view his work at http://photo.kphyfe.com) and raising awareness for other veterans who need service dogs.

As a life member of the National Organization of Veterans' Advocates, Inc., Disabled Veterans of America, and the American Legion, Phyfe's newfound purpose in life is helping other veterans. "If I can help raise money for another veteran, it gives me purpose in life," says Phyfe.

Once isolated, housebound, and on the edge of suicide, Phyfe has logged more than 27,000 miles advocating on behalf of AVD and the benefits of service dogs for wounded veterans—all with Iris by his side. Phyfe's goal is to raise enough money to pay for the training of three or four service dogs per year, which is an admirable goal, considering that the average cost to raise and train one service dog is roughly $25,000 to $50,000 (guide dogs average between $50,000 and $70,000). Additionally, Phyfe is a member of the AVD speakers' bureau and serves on the alumni council for both AVD and the Guide Dog Foundation for the Blind.

"All of this and so much more has happened because of this little rescue out of Georgia who has become my rescuer," says Phyfe. "The gift of living was given back to me. I still have all of the medical issues, but I no longer want to die. I want to live and be part of this world. There is no way to really say 'thank you' to America's VetDogs for all they have done for me other than to live the life they have given back to me."

Kent and Mike went through training in real-life situations.

At nearly eight years old, Iris officially retired on May 17, 2015. As an advocate for service dogs, Phyfe has been involved in helping AVD and its joint project with the Department of Corrections' Prison Puppy Program at Enfield Correctional Institution, Enfield, Connecticut, since its inception. Dogs graduating from prison programs go on to receive advanced training prior to being paired with veterans.

Although Phyfe knew that his new dog would come from a prison program, he didn't know which prison. "For me, it has special meaning," says Phyfe. "To have been involved with the VetDogs prison program and see how it helps change communities and the prisoners is icing on the cake."

Nearly one year after applying for a replacement service dog, and only one day prior to officially retiring Iris, Phyfe received a new dog. Mike, a seventeen-month-old English Labrador Retriever, weighing in at a lean 74 pounds, has already put his sharp instinct and ability to sense Phyfe's distress to work. The first night, while

training at AVD's training center, Phyfe's heart went into arrhythmia, and Mike gently nudged Phyfe's face to wake him. "That's not a behavior that can be trained," says Phyfe. "It's intuitive. You can only train him to react. He knew the first night that something was going on." Once Phyfe assured Mike that he was fine, Mike let him go back to sleep.

On the third night of training, Mike pulled the covers off Phyfe, which is how AVD trains dogs to handle nightmare interruption. "It woke me up, and I acknowledged him with a big 'Yes!' He was all wiggles and kisses."

New to Phyfe is a small medical-alert device that attaches to his belt loop. Should Phyfe's heart go into arrhythmia while in public, causing him to pass out, Mike is trained to locate the device and pull the tab, which triggers a loud, shrill noise designed to attract people. Mike is trained to then lie down next to Phyfe until help arrives or Phyfe releases him.

"Mike lies down next to me because some people can be afraid of dogs—especially large dogs like Mike," says Phyfe. "Having him in a *down* position is the least aggressive position and safest place for him." During the training phase, the trainers incorporated people walking up and talking to Phyfe, which conditioned Mike to having strangers approach and reinforced Mike's behavior of staying next to Phyfe.

As with Iris, Phyfe uses a cross-body shoulder harness rather than a leash to walk Mike. Several crushed vertebrae from multiple deployments often trigger numbness in his hand and arm, and, should he inadvertently drop the leash or pass out, Mike is always close by.

Most amazingly, like Iris, Mike is trained to push a button inside Phyfe's home that is a direct line to 911. But unlike Iris, Mike must initially determine that Phyfe is at home. He

Attacks on Guide Dogs

Like George (see page 160), who was attacked and permanently removed from guide work, Iris was attacked by dogs on two different occasions over the course of four years, which may have hastened her retirement. One attack happened while Phyfe and Iris were walking in their neighborhood, doing volunteer work. The second incident occurred while they were riding the train on their way to a public-awareness radio interview with Sean Hannity. Phyfe recounts how a fake service dog jumped off the seat across the aisle from him and bit Iris.

Most unbelievably, service dogs being attacked by pet dogs or fake service dogs is not uncommon. In fact, the statistics are alarming. While data regarding attacks in the United States are not available, the Guide Dogs for the Blind Association in the United Kingdom published a 2013 report indicating the following:

• A total of 240 dog attacks on guide dogs between March 2011 and February 2013 were reported. This is an average of ten attacks per month and an increase from the 2012 statistics, which showed an average of eight attacks per month.

• Five of the dogs attacked in the two-year period were permanently withdrawn from service, costing the nonprofit guide-dog organization an estimated £171,657, which equates to roughly $264,000 in today's market.

• Roughly one-quarter of the dogs attacked from 2011 to 2013 had been attacked before, and, of those, 26 percent had been attacked by the same dog.

• Twenty-two percent of the time, the aggressor dogs were not with their owners.

• Forty-two percent of the aggressor dogs were with their owners but not on leash.

does this by first checking Phyfe's belt loop for the medical alert, which Phyfe always wears when outside. If it's there, Mike is trained to pull the tab that activates the shrill noise. If it's not there, he knows to hit the indoor button that connects to 911 and then lie next to Phyfe until paramedics arrive (911 responds to calls with no response).

In terms of service dogs, Iris and Mike are worlds apart. Mike is physically bigger, more energetic, a natural retriever, and not the least bit aggressive toward other dogs. Mike is selectively bred for service-dog work and part of AVD's Prison Puppy Program—raised and trained by inmates. Iris, also trained by AVD, is a rescued shelter dog—her pedigree and history unknown. Yet, retiring Iris has stirred mixed emotions for Phyfe—a difficult decision that was distressing, yet insightful. For four years, Iris walked by Phyfe's side as a certified service dog and best friend. Today, her service days are over. She currently lives with Phyfe's son and spends her days being a dog. A happy, silly dog—playing, soaking up the sun, and relaxing, which has made the decision easier for Phyfe.

"Iris saved my life, and I felt like I was letting her down. But the staff at AVD was so instrumental in helping me get through the process without the guilt of feeling like I was leaving a good friend, when in fact I was helping her by letting her off the hook from working when she was stressing to stay on the job."

As one journey ends, another begins. A bittersweet time of profound memories, tough decisions, golden chances, and future opportunities. With Mike by his side, Phyfe plans to continue traveling, advocating, educating, and spreading the word about service dogs for injured veterans. "I can never say thank you enough for what America's VetDogs has done for me—twice."

3

GUIDE DOGS

GUIDE DOGS

According to an article titled "The Seeing Eye," written by The Seeing Eye co-founder Dorothy Harrison Eustis and published in the November 5, 1927, *Saturday Evening Post,* the cost of training a guide dog at that time was about $60, which included the initial cost of the dog. Today, with an average price tag of $50,000 (some experts suggest as high as $70,000) to breed, raise, and train one guide dog, these canines undergo a comprehensive training program that only the best of the best complete.

Guide dogs, once referred to as "blind guides," can be traced to the first century AD and the buried ruins of the ancient Roman town Herculaneum, according to the article "History of Guide Dogs" on the International Guide Dog Federation's website (www.igdf.org.uk). An article titled "The History of Guide Dogs in Britain" from the Guide Dogs (UK) website (*www.guidedogs.org.uk*) tells of early examples of European art that depict the blind accompanied by dogs. Stories are told of an eighteenth-century Parisian hospital for the blind that attempted to train guide dogs, while a blind sieve-maker in Vienna was said to have trained a dog so effectively for his own use that people thought he was sighted.

Training on the streets of Lausanne, Switzerland, with German Shepherd guide-dog candidates.

Military dogs deployed by the French Legion during World War I who were unable to fulfill their combat duties for various reasons, including injury, were retrained to be the companions of blind ex-soldiers. Despite the accessibility of dogs, however, it was not a very popular service because, according to Ernest Harold Baynes, author of *Animal Heroes of the Great War* (1925), of "the feeling that a blind man led by a dog must necessarily appear to be an object of charity."

The modern guide dog story really begins during World War I when the Germans—always way ahead of the game when it came to breeding, raising, and training dogs—assigned German Shepherd Dogs to soldiers who had been blinded by mustard gas. The aforementioned article "History of Guide Dogs" tells us that German physician Dr. Gerhard Stalling was walking the grounds of a veterans' hospital with a blind patient. Called away suddenly, Dr. Stalling left his German Shepherd Dog with the patient to keep him company. Upon returning, he believed that the dog had been looking after the patient, trying to help him. Thereafter, Stalling began

exploring ways of training dogs to become guides, and, in 1916, he opened a guide-dog school in Oldenburg. The facility shut down within a decade, but by then a large guide-dog school in Potsdam, near Berlin, had opened. The school was capable of accommodating around 100 dogs at a time and providing up to twelve fully trained guide dogs per month. In its first eighteen years, the article states, the school "trained over 2,500 dogs with a rejection rate of just 6 percent."

The guide-dog school came to the attention of Dorothy Harrison Eustis, a wealthy American dog breeder living in Switzerland who, at the time, was interested in the scientific breeding of German Shepherd Dogs for the desirable characteristics of alertness, responsibility, and stamina. Eustis, a breeder and trainer of German Shepherds for the army, police, and Red Cross, saw firsthand how the Germans were rehabilitating their "war blind" and was impressed by what she witnessed at the school. It forever changed her way of thinking about the future of blind people. She began to think more broadly, wondering if selective breeding could develop guide-dog qualities more widely. If so, why not selectively breed and train dogs to assist the blind?

Eustis's previously mentioned *Saturday Evening Post* article changed the lives of the blind everywhere. She wrote:

> *In darkness and uncertainty he must start again, wholly dependent on outside help for every move. His other senses may rally to his aid, but they cannot replace his sight. To man's never failing friend has accord this special privilege. Gentlemen, I give you the German shepherd dog...*
>
> *No longer dependent on a member of the family, a friend, or a paid attendant, the blind can once more take up their normal lives as nearly possible where they left them off...*
>
> *That crowds and traffic have no longer any terrors for him and that his evenings can be spent among friends without responsibility or burden to them.*

The article caught the attention of Mr. Frank of Nashville, Tennessee, who read it to his nineteen-year-old blind son, Morris. The young man had lost his sight in one eye in 1914 during a riding accident when he was six years old. Ten years later, his other eye was damaged beyond repair in a high school boxing match.

Morris Frank wrote to Mrs. Eustis, asking her to train a dog to help him. In April 1928, he set sail for Europe, accepting Eustis's invitation to visit her school and see about a guide dog for himself. Before guide dogs, people who were blind were simply marginalized. Few, if any, provisions for them existed. Such was the case with Morris Frank, who, because he could not fend for himself on his travels overseas, was deemed a "package" rather than a passenger. The crew went so far as to restrict his movement, and he was not permitted to leave his room to move about the ship without someone from the ship's staff accompanying him, writes Kate Kelly in "The First Seeing Eye Dog Is Used in America in 1928" on her America Comes Alive! website (*www.americacomesalive.com*).

Not far from Eustis's Fortunate Fields kennel in the Swiss Alps, Frank was paired with a German Shepherd Dog named Kiss, although he quickly changed the dog's name to Buddy because, as the story goes, he could not imagine calling out, "Come, Kiss!"

Within weeks, Frank, with Buddy in harness, was smoothly and confidently navigating the streets of Vevey, Switzerland. Returning home, Frank and Buddy disembarked in New York City, where they were greeted dockside by a crowd of spectators, reporters, and photographers. On a dare from one of the reporters, Frank instructed Buddy to cross

Morris Frank with Buddy, who would later become a national heroine.

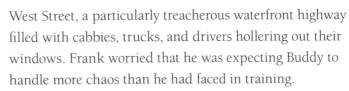

West Street, a particularly treacherous waterfront highway filled with cabbies, trucks, and drivers hollering out their windows. Frank worried that he was expecting Buddy to handle more chaos than he had faced in training.

As Frank stepped from the curb, he put his life in his dog's training. He surrendered all control to Buddy, and, for three long minutes, Frank was completely directionless. Upon reaching the other side, he wrapped his arms around Buddy and praised her: "Good, good girl!" She had done her job. As a trained guide dog, she had become Frank's eyes, able to safely guide him across a hectic intersection.

Later that day, Frank sent a one-word telegram to Eustis: "Success!" Eustis soon left Switzerland for America, with her arrival noted in the *New York Times*: "Shepherd Dogs Coming for American Blind." The article goes on to describe that Mrs. Dorothy Harrison Eustis was sailing with three German Shepherd Dogs, which were "the first contingent of the great canine army which will eventually go to the United States as leaders of the blind."

In 1929, Eustis and Frank helped establish The Seeing

Frank trusted Buddy to lead him across crowded, busy city streets.

The first graduating class
of The Seeing Eye in 1929.

Eye in Nashville, Tennessee—the first guide-dog program in the United States. Eight years and 50,000 miles later, Frank and Buddy had traveled by foot, train, subway, bus, and boat, preaching and demonstrating the life-changing aspects of having a guide dog. By 1936, 250 dogs had been paired with blind men and women in the United States. Today, The Seeing Eye's campus is in Morristown, New Jersey, and it remains the oldest existing guide-dog school in the world.

The day after Japan bombed Pearl Harbor—December 8, 1941—The Seeing Eye's trustees resolved to supply without charge guide dogs to veterans of World War II if they needed them. By then, Buddy had passed away (she was hailed as a national heroine when she died in 1938), but Frank and Buddy II were touring Army, Navy, and Veterans Administration hospitals to tout the benefits of guide dogs.

Today's metropolitan environment is more complex than ever, and the criteria and standards for guide dogs—those magnificent canine humanitarians—remain as high, if not higher, than they did in the late 1920s when Dorothy Harrison Eustis started The Seeing Eye school. Those same requisite qualities that she described in her 1927 article—courage, intelligence, steady nerves—are equally important to today's guide dogs.

All sorts of dogs can become guide dogs, but popular breeds for today's guide work are Labrador Retrievers, Golden Retrievers, and Labrador/Golden Retriever crosses, which combine the best traits of each breed and are favored for their size and strength. German Shepherd Dogs, while not quite as popular today, are still trained, as are some Standard Poodles, but Labrador Retrievers are the most

A five-week-old future guide-dog trainee from a line of Labrador Retrievers selectively bred for the work.

Future guide dogs must meet all specified health requirements.

frequently used breed anywhere in the world as guide dogs, according to Brad Hibbard, Director of Training Operations for Guide Dogs for the Blind, a training school with campuses in California and Oregon.

While some organizations utilize shelter dogs, the majority of guide dogs are selectively bred from generations of proven breeding stock for their calm, loyal, intelligent temperaments and their proven track record as guide dogs. While other breeds may possess the requisite traits, dogs must be adaptable to all environments. Unfortunately, breed stereotypes exist, and a blind person getting on a bus or train with a gentle yet intimidating-looking American Pit Bull Terrier or Rottweiler, for example, is likely to have some passengers searching for the closest exit. While other breeds, such as the Boxer and Doberman Pinscher, have been used in the past, their short coats often preclude them from working in colder climates.

Additionally, guide dogs must possess good environmental confidence in chaotic settings, such as downtown Manhattan or San Francisco or smaller urban neighborhoods. Granted, all dogs have some degree of environmental stimulation, but it is a question of degree. For example, a car backfiring or a door slamming may startle a guide dog working in downtown Los Angeles. How quickly does he recover? How long does it take him to get back to work? A few seconds? Or does he remain started, worried, or distracted? Likewise, a handler would be ill-served by a Labrador Retriever who darts into traffic to chase a bird or a Golden Retriever who stops to pick up every stick or ball that crosses his path.

Before a potential guide dog receives specialized training, he must master the basic commands.

Before a guide dog is matched with a handler, a lot of time and money is involved. Future guide dogs are earmarked from puppyhood and start their training early—as early as one week old—with trainers regularly holding and touching them so they quickly learn to be comfortable with people. Around four to five weeks of age, the puppies are exposed to leash training as well as to different noises, toys, and surfaces, such as grass, concrete, sand, dirt, gravel, tile, and so forth. At about nine weeks of age, puppies go to volunteer puppy raisers

until they are about fourteen months old. Interestingly, more and more puppies are being raised and trained through prison puppy programs, as discussed in Chapter 2.

In a safe and positive environment—and following detailed guidelines provided by the guide-dog organization—puppy raisers provide each puppy with housetraining, basic obedience, and socialization, introducing the puppy to all of the sights and sounds that he is likely to encounter as an adult dog. It is important for the puppy to meet other animals, kids on bicycles, women in floppy hats, men with mustaches, and so forth. He should see and hear the clapping of hands, the vacuum cleaner, the microwave, and the like. He should go up and down stairs and elevators. Throughout the socialization process, puppies are carefully and regularly monitored for any quirks or traits that might preclude them from future guide-dog work. Some puppies may be too soft or too independent, so it takes a lot more work to mold them into future guide dogs.

In most training programs, the dogs spend a little more than a year with their puppy-raiser families, after which they undergo various assessments.

Around fourteen to sixteen months of age, the dogs are returned to the guide-dog facility, where instructors again carefully assess their personalities, temperaments, confidence, concentration, and other important traits.

Positive motivation and reinforcement training allow trainers to complete a guide dog's specialized training in about ten weeks. Before being assigned to a person who is blind, a guide dog must have perfect obedience skills, yet he cannot be a machine. He must obey all commands, yet be ready to take matters into his own paws should the handler's command pitch them into danger; this is known as *intelligent disobedience*— dogs are trained to ignore or refuse commands that may lead their handlers into danger, such as crossing a street with oncoming traffic. By disregarding the command and taking initiative, the dog gives warning to the handler and usually averts disaster, as was the case with Cpl. Michael Jernigan and

On-campus training at Southeastern Guide Dogs.

his guide dog Brittani (see page 78), who disobeyed her handler's *forward* command because she saw the electrically powered Toyota Prius that Jernigan could not hear.

Part of a guide dog's specialized training is learning to walk in a straight line until he encounters a reason to stop, such as an obstacle or intersection, and then wait for the handler's command. Dogs are trained to identify changes in sidewalk elevations—those cutaways in sidewalks that indicate a curb or intersection—and to stop at these changes in elevation.

Obviously, a dog can't tell a red light from a green light, so how does he know when to cross a busy street? His handler tells him when to cross. Handlers use their auditory skills—listening to the flow of cross-traffic—to determine when it's safe to cross. Try it yourself. Stand on the corner of a busy intersection and close your eyes. What do you hear? Car horns,

Dottie litter puppy golden lab walking on playground.

traffic patterns, the shuffle and flow of pedestrians? Can you hear when traffic stops? With your eyes still closed, imagine crossing the intersection without stepping into traffic.

While a dog may eventually learn his human partner's daily routines, the handler ultimately directs the dog with a series of *forward*, *left*, and *right* commands. Specially designed GPS devices are helping blind handlers navigate unfamiliar cities. By programming the intended location into the device, a handler knows when and for how long to continue forward and when to turn left or right.

At the same time, a blind person isn't able to see any obstructions or barriers along the route, such as low-hanging branches or wires, potholes, telephone or light poles, concrete barriers, and so forth. Just as they are trained to stop at intersections, guide dogs are also trained to stop when faced with an obstruction.

In a newsletter published by Guide Dogs for the Blind, Bonnie Cursey, the niece of World War II veteran Sgt. Leonard Faulk, who lost his sight when his binoculars were hit by sniper fire at the Battle of Attu and was the first veteran to graduate from the program with a guide dog, recounts a story about intelligent disobedience. In the article, Cursey talks about the defining moment when Faulk really developed a "blind trust" in his guide dog, Blondie. It came as they were walking in a familiar place in San Francisco, and Faulk doubted one of Blondie's actions. "Blondie did something to indicate that Leonard should move over, and he ignored her. Urging her forward, Blondie once again tried to signal Leonard to move over. He ignored her yet again, and as they moved forward at his insistence, Leonard ran right into a light pole, striking his head." Cursey told the writer of the article that it was the one and only time that her uncle ignored Blondie's signals.

Once a dog and handler have been matched, the final stages of training occur when they train together. Generally, although not always, this consists of a twenty-six-day

Dogs for the Blind

Guide Dogs for the Blind in San Rafael, California, is one of less than a dozen organizations in the United States that breed, raise, and train guide dogs. Of the roughly 800 puppies bred each year by the nonprofit, roughly 60 percent (about 480 puppies per year) go on to become successful guide dogs, according to Pat Cook, Guide Dogs for the Blind's canine resources manager. They currently have more than 2,100 canine graduates working in the field as guide dogs.

training period during which dog and handler live and train together on the organization's campus. They learn how to become a team, how to navigate the real world, and all of the various commands necessary for the handler to live a more independent life. Often, if a handler has previously had a guide dog and is receiving a new one, he or she will complete a two-week home placement rather than the twenty-six-day on-campus course.

Occasionally, during training, it becomes clear that a dog does not possess the traits necessary to be an effective guide

David Caporali with his guide dog Doc, thanks to Southeastern Guide Dogs.

Guide-Dog Etiquette

Working guide dogs, as well as service dogs, should be ignored by the public because distractions take their focus and concentration away from their important jobs. Please keep these tips in mind when in the presence of a guide dog to allow for the safety of the dog and his handler:

- This is a working dog, not a pet. Do not touch, talk to, feed, or otherwise distract the dog while he is wearing his harness. Some handlers will allow petting, but always ask first.

- A distracted dog can result in a life-or-death situation for the handler.

- Speak to the handler, not to the dog.

- Guide-dog teams have the right of way. Assist the handler if he or she requests help; otherwise, do not try to take control.

- Do not grab the dog's harness or grab or steer the person while the dog is working. Ask if the handler needs assistance. If so, offer your left arm.

- When walking with a guide dog, ask the handler where you should walk, such as on the handler's right side, slightly ahead of the handler, or behind the handler. Walking on the dog's left side may be confusing and/or distracting.

dog. This can be due to an inability to focus, too much energy for the job, or the tendency to be too easily stimulated, distracted, or overreactive. In some cases, the dog may develop unforeseen medical issues, such as such as hip dysplasia, cataracts, chronic car sickness, or severe allergies, during training.

Prior to placement, trainers evaluate and try to match the handler's temperament, personality, and activity level with that of the dog. They also look at the person's gait—walking pattern, pace/speed—as well as the person's age, energy level, his or her ability to manage the needs of a dog (i.e., the dog's drive, energy, size, strength, etc.), and, finally, the environment the dog will be working in, be it in rural areas with trails or unpaved surfaces or crowded, noisy, chaotic city sidewalks and streets with plenty of traffic.

Although precise numbers are not available, Guiding Eyes for the Blind's website states that an estimated 10,000 guide-dog teams are currently working in the United States. Interestingly, not all dogs work equally well for all people. Mismatches happen, and some

Hearing Dogs

Back in the early 1970s, Elva Janke, a hearing-impaired woman in Minnesota, had a dog who had instinctively learned to alert her to the sounds that she could not hear. As Janke's hearing failed even further, the dog would alert her to more and more sounds. When Janke's dog passed away, she realized how dependent she had become on him, and she went in search of someone to train another dog to do the same thing. Ruth Deschene, then the executive director of the Minnesota Humane Society, found dog trainer Agnes McGrath, who began training a dog for Janke, and eventually she trained the first six hearing dogs in Minnesota. The training program was transferred to the American Humane Association's (AHA) headquarters in Denver, Colorado, and eventually Hearing Dog, Inc., was formed by McGrath as a separate, independent nonprofit organization. After training and placing its first dog in Canada, the 501(c)(3) organization was renamed International Hearing Dog, Inc.

At around the same time, the AHA contacted Roy Kabat, who trained exotic animals for the movies. After spending two weeks in Denver, Kabat returned to Oregon and founded Dogs for the Deaf, Inc., a 501 (c)(3) organization that still trains dogs on its 40-acre campus.

It's impossible to say with any certainty how many organizations today train dogs for the deaf or hearing impaired, or how many people use these dogs. In his book *Service and Therapy Dogs in American Society,* author John Ensminger notes that, in 2001, there were an estimated 4,000 hearing dogs in the United States and at least fifty facilities training hearing dogs.

Hearing, or signal, dogs alert their handlers to specific sounds, primarily in the home, such as a doorbell ringing, alarm clock beeping, smoke or security alarm screeching, tea kettle whistling, telephone ringing, or baby crying. These dogs let their owners know when someone is calling the owner's name or when the computer makes a sound to signal that they've received e-mail. Some dogs naturally learn to alert to common household noises, such as the clothes dryer or microwave buzzer.

Typically, dogs are trained to get their owners' attention—usually by running toward the sound, then running back to the owner, then running back to the sound, and so forth. If the owner is sleeping or not paying attention, the dog may nose-bump, nudge, or paw at the person. Barking is generally discouraged because the deaf person isn't going to hear it, and barking is often associated with canine territorial issues. For smoke alarms, the dog is usually trained to jump on the bed to wake the person, who must then determine why he or she has been awakened.

Most formally trained hearing dogs respond to at least four sounds. Once a dog is matched to a deaf or hearing-impaired handler, a trainer works with the dog and handler to reinforce the alerting behavior. Some dogs' training is customized to match the person's lifestyle and living conditions.

The majority of dogs are trained for use in the owner's home, as opposed to "signaling" in public. Some organizations train dogs to respond to sirens, honking horns, and the like; however, most often, the dogs are naturally paying attention to things happening around them. A hearing-dog owner eventually understands and becomes accustomed to his or her dog's natural reactions to sounds while in public. In turn, this causes the owner to become more aware of his or her environment and eventually learn to look in the direction of the sounds that the dog focuses on.

Unlike guide or service dogs, which are generally Labrador Retrievers, Golden Retrievers, Golden/Lab crosses, or medium-to-large rescue dogs, hearing dogs are often small purebred or mixed-breed dogs, including shelter dogs, who are often favored for their compact size because they can jump onto their owners' laps, if necessary, to get their attention.

Guide dogs are trained to navigate different types of terrain and surfaces.

dogs end up being returned to the guide-dog organization after placement. At Guide Dogs for the Blind, about 10 percent of the dogs end up coming back to the organization within the first twelve months. Of those 10 percent, about 25 percent of the dogs are rematched with different handlers.

Dogs who are dropped from the program often go on to work as medical alert/response dogs (e.g., seizure- or diabetes-response dogs). Some dogs are donated to military or law-enforcement agencies to be trained as search-and-rescue, drug-detection, or explosives-detection dogs. Others go on to become emotional-support or therapy dogs at hospitals or nursing homes. Some of the dogs assist people who are deaf or hard of hearing. Others go back to their original puppy-raisers and live out their lives as cherished companions.

MICHAEL JERNIGAN & BRITTANI

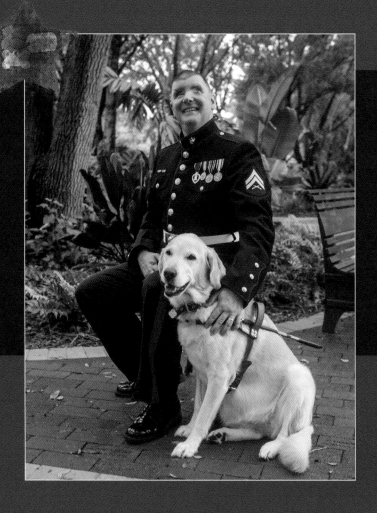

Independence is recognizing the obstacles in front of you, making the necessary adaptations, and moving forward with the knowledge that although some journeys are more difficult than others, none of them are impossible.

~ Michael Jernigan

"If Brittani had not blocked my path into the street, I'd be dead. I'd be a hood ornament on a Toyota Prius. Not a manly way to die for a man who survived three roadside bombs."

One can't help but smile as retired Marine Cpl. Michael Jernigan, with his oversized and colorful personality, shares dozens of stories about life with his guide dog Brittani, a gorgeous Golden Retriever/Labrador Retriever mix that embodies the best qualities of both breeds—affection, devotion, intelligence, and loyalty.

The young Marine
in his dress blues.

Jernigan explains how, on that particular day, he was leaving the Institute of World Politics, a graduate school in the DuPont Circle area of Washington DC, heading toward the metro station to catch a cab. Standing on a street corner, Jernigan listened for cross-traffic noise. Hearing none, he gave Brittani her command to cross the street. She disobeyed. She just stood there. Jernigan gave another *forward* command. This time, Brittani took one step forward and then stepped directly in front of Jernigan, blocking his movement into the street. Simultaneously, a whoosh of air blew past Jernigan. Brittani had done her job. She had kept him from stepping into the path of an electric car—a car that makes zero noise. A car Jernigan couldn't hear.

In what is known as "intelligent disobedience," guide dogs are trained to ignore or refuse a command that may lead their handlers into danger, just like Brittani did in that instance. By disregarding their handlers' commands and taking their own initiative, guide dogs give warning to their handlers and usually avert disaster.

"She did what she was trained to do," explains Jernigan. "She disobeyed my command because she knew something that I did not. She could see the car that I could not hear. That day, she literally saved my life. Had I been traveling with just a white cane, I would have stepped out into the street and become a large hood ornament. 'Marine survives three roadside bombs and numerous fire fights to come home and get hit by a Toyota Prius!'"

Brittani has been Michael's eyes as well as a strong source of emotional support.

August 22, 2004. Two years into his military service and six months into a seven-month deployment, twenty-five-year-old Jernigan and four fellow Marines were on patrol south of Baghdad, on the outskirts of Mahmudiya, when a roadside bomb tore through their Humvee. "We were cruising down the street and, all of a sudden, 'boom!' I was blown 20 meters out of the vehicle."

The explosion killed one Marine and injured the others, with Jernigan being the most severely wounded. The IED crushed 45 percent of his forehead, took out both of his eyes, and left him with a TBI. The blast also crushed his right hand, tore open an artery in his left leg, and severely injured his knee. In less than a second, the trajectory of Jernigan's life changed forever.

Jernigan was med-evaced to the 31st Combat Support Hospital in Baghdad and then transferred to Landstuhl Regional Medical Center in Germany, the largest American hospital outside the United States, where he underwent multiple surgeries to stabilize a very touch-and-go situation. His father, retired Maj. Michael V. Jernigan, was a few hours away in Stuttgart and rushed to his son's side.

While Jernigan was still in the Baghdad hospital, Jernigan's godfather, an Army colonel, had held a satellite phone next to Jernigan's ear as his mother, Tracey Willis, spoke to him from half a world away while he remained in a medically induced coma. "I learned that during these times, my blood pressure would rise," says Jernigan. "The doctor said that it was a good sign—it meant I had some brain activity."

Shortly thereafter, Jernigan was transferred to the National Naval Medical Center in Bethesda, Maryland. After his recovery, he was sent to the VA hospital in Tampa, Florida, where he was evaluated and treated for his TBI. He then completed a sixteen-week blind rehabilitation course at the VA hospital in Augusta, Georgia.

"I now rock some wicked cool scars that include a 14-inch long one that runs from temple to temple across the top of my head. I still wear a regulation high and tight haircut, and all my friends tell me I should grow my hair out. My chest puffs out, and I tell them, 'You don't need medals when you have scars like mine,'" says Jernigan, recipient of both the Purple Heart and Combat Action Ribbon.

Jernigan jokes about the visible scars, as well as his collection of five prosthetic eyes, including a diamond-studded one that he has been known to pop out and show to inquisitive kids. He jokes now, but his recovery was long and tedious, including thirty major surgeries in the first twelve months and sixteen months in hospitals and rehabilitation facilities. His marriage fell apart, and the invisible wounds—the deep emotional wounds—associated with PTSD took their toll as well. He drank too much. He had trouble sleeping. He was angry. He had nightmares. He dropped into a severe depression. His life was in disarray.

Just a few months earlier, he had been a physically fit United States Marine serving in a war as an infantry assaultman—"the greatest fighting force on the face of the planet." Military service was in his blood. His father had retired as a major in the United States Army after serving in the Vietnam War, and his grandfather had retired as a colonel after twenty-eight years of service. Being a Marine was the first job that Jernigan was truly proud of. Losing his independence and relying on others for everything he needed was a difficult and problematic adjustment—the hardest part of his recovery.

Ironically, his penchant for fine cigars put him on the path to restoring his soul and getting his life back on track. A chance encounter at his favorite cigar haunt led him to Bobby Newman, a Southeastern Guide Dogs board member. In late 2005, Newman and Jernigan came up with the idea for Paws For Patriots, a Southeastern Guide Dog program designed to serve the needs of disabled veterans from all eras who have honorably served our country. In January 2006, Jernigan made the donation that got Paws For Patriots started, and, on March 28, 2007, he was paired with Brittani, becoming the first veteran to receive a service dog through the newly founded program. "Brittani is my angel," says Jernigan. "She came into my life when I needed more than a guide dog. I needed guidance. Without her, I'd be at the bottom of a bottle of Johnnie Walker or possibly dead.

"I will always remember March 28, 2007, as one of the best days of my life. It was on the Southeastern campus in Palmetto, Florida. I was eagerly awaiting a knock on the door of my private room. When I heard the knock, I got very excited. I opened the door and was greeted by trainer Kate Perez and a lovely yellow [dog] named Brittani. We were introduced and then left alone to get to know each other. She was excited to see me, and I was ecstatic to see her. Her tail was wagging so fast that her butt was moving back and forth. I knew right then that she was the dog for me."

On a side note, Jernigan was just two months shy of his twenty-sixth birthday when he lost his vision. With his speech already conditioned, he chooses not to adjust his vocabulary because he is blind, so he still uses words such as *see*, *watch*, and *view*. "I guess I do not feel that I should have to use different language just because things are different," he says. "I am still the same, except for the sight, but I was not a great driver anyway!"

After completing the twenty-six-day training program on Southeastern's campus, Jernigan and Brittani boarded a flight home to Washington, DC, where the real journey began. Prior to joining the Marines, Jernigan had spent four and a half years as a freshman at a local college—not for lack of intelligence but rather out of lack of discipline and enthusiasm. Dropping out of college, he bid farewell to academia and his 1.16 GPA. "College was the only thing I had ever given up on," says Jernigan.

Medically retired from the military, Jernigan looked at his options and decided that "a blind man with no college degree didn't have much opportunity." Drawing upon the Marine Corps' "never quit" mentality, and with the love and support of his family, Jernigan started to put his fractured life back together.

Three years and one day after being blown up and nearly losing his life to a roadside bomb some 8,000 miles from his Virginia home, Jernigan, with Brittani by his side, enrolled at Northern Virginia Community College, eventually transferring to Georgetown University. Yes, *that* Georgetown University—one of the world's leading academic and research institutions.

Founded in 1789, a lot of the original buildings are still in use, but many of those 200-year-old buildings lack Braille and tactile signs on their doors, which caused Jernigan a good deal of stress. Those raised letters that mark doors and elevators help blind students like Jernigan find their classrooms as well as tell them what floor they are on and what direction they need to travel to get to where they need to go. Absent tactile signs, navigating some areas of campus further stressed Jernigan's already stressed life. After one year at Georgetown, he transferred to the University of South Florida St. Petersburg and graduated with a bachelor's degree in history. "Brittani helped me find my classes and helped me stay calm in loud, crowded hallways that kept my anxiety level at an eight," says Jernigan. "She was there to let me know that we could do it together. With her, I could do anything."

Brittani traveled beside Jernigan every step of the way, including at Georgetown, when an encounter in Red Square, the center of student-life activities, sent his anxiety and stress levels skyrocketing. For veterans struggling with PTSD, tightly packed crowds can trigger anger and fear and send tempers flaring.

That day, the day after the 2008 presidential election, Jernigan was heading to Georgetown University Hospital to catch a cab. Doing so meant crossing Red Square, which was packed with hundreds of students. With Brittani at his side, Jernigan pushed his way through the crowd but came out on the other side emotionally agitated and visibly distressed. His temperature was elevated, and he was sweating despite the November chill. Continuing toward the hospital, Brittani abruptly stopped—just as she had been trained to do when encountering an obstacle. Jernigan searched for one in front of him—first with his left foot, then his right. Nothing. As he continued searching, Brittani bumped his left hand with her cold nose. "What's wrong, Brittani?"

he asked as he went down on one knee, scratching her behind the ears. Suddenly, his "angel" was wagging her tail. Once again, Brittani's natural instincts kicked in. She'd done her job of calming Jernigan.

Brittani's training and natural instinct are hardwired to Jernigan's moods. She displays astonishing instinct at reading his body language and detecting his elevated heart rate, temperature, anxiety, and stress levels. She's confident, experienced. She knows what to do, and again she did her job by bringing Jernigan back to the present and defusing potentially explosive emotions lurking just below the boiling point. It was a perfectly emblematic moment, representative of what Brittani does for Jernigan on a daily basis.

"I'm a thirty-six-year-old third-generation combat Marine," says Jernigan. "If you'd have told me fifteen years ago that a dog could have that much impact on a man's pride, I would have had you drug-tested."

In that moment, Jernigan realized that Brittani was much more than just a guide dog. Whether he is working on daily tasks at home, navigating the city, or staying in a hotel room, Brittani is his anchor. She supports him twenty-four hours a day, seven days a week, and she knows how he is feeling at all times. She knows what he needs more than he does. Her work is neither simple nor easy; she just makes it look that way. Her training and profound communication skills coupled with her natural canine instincts are effective far beyond any human's capabilities. "When I travel by myself, I am never truly alone. Brittani is always by my side," says Jernigan.

A passionate and tireless advocate for injured veterans, Jernigan has crisscrossed the country with Brittani—from navigating the halls of Congress in our nation's capital to meandering the eclectic thoroughfare known as Santa Monica Boulevard, with its fancy boutiques, lively cafés and restaurants, and larger-than-life public art exhibits. They have strolled Yankee Stadium, the gaming floors of Caesar's Palace, and countless points in between.

Today, with a university diploma in hand, Jernigan returned to where it all began—Southeastern Guide Dogs, where he works as a donor-relations manager.

"Brittani saved me from the bottle, she saved me from electric cars, but, most importantly, Brittani saved me from the demons that haunt a significant amount of our combat veterans. Brittani walked by my side for eight years, pointing me in the right direction, keeping me safe, and making sure that I was loved. It is that unconditional love that only can come from an animal. Brittani saved my life. Brittani kept me sane. Brittani became the best friend I could have ever asked for, and she is my angel."

When Brittani is not hard at work, you can find her hard at play.

In February 2015—after eight years of walking by Jernigan's side, changing his life with her highly specialized training, keen intelligence, natural instinct, loyalty, single-minded devotion, and easygoing presence, Brittani retired at the age of ten. Her service days are over, and Jernigan is waiting to be matched with a new guide dog from Southeastern Guide Dogs. Today, Brittani lives nearby with the family of one of Jernigan's good friends. She spends her days soaking up the Florida sunshine, swimming, and playing with the family's three-year-old son. "She's very happy," says Jernigan, "and that's made it easier for me. She's one of the most amazing dogs on the face of the planet."

BRIAN K. PEARCE
&
OTHELLO

To give the blind man a seeing eye is a very great boon; but to give him along with it a loyal, faithful, dependable, courageous, and affectionate comrade, who will lay down his life for his friend without whimper or hesitation, is to make the world somehow a really better place.

~ Raymond Pearl, 1937

Eight years after awaking from a medically induced coma and wondering, "What the heck is my wife doing in Iraq?," retired Army Staff Sergeant Brian Pearce committed himself to giving back to the organization that helped him regain his independence, thereby saving his life.

Pearce had not planned on a military career, but after being laid off from the sheriff's department in his Ohio hometown, the twenty-three-year-old enlisted in 1992—right after Operation Desert Storm—deploying to Somalia, Bosnia, and Honduras before his contract ended in 2000. Returning to work as a police officer, Pearce also spent a year and a half in the Army Reserves and a year in the National Guard. Working three jobs to support his family proved too much, so Pearce re-enlisted in the army in 2003. Shortly thereafter, he was posted to Fort Wainright, Alaska, before being deployed to Mosul, Iraq, in 2005, as part of the 172nd Stryker Brigade Combat Team.

Brian on the job during his deployment to Iraq.

Brian and a pair of local Iraqi boys give the thumbs up.

In-country for one year, Pearce's unit was scheduled to return home, but his deployment was extended. In 2006, his unit was sent to the Sunni Triangle (a densely populated region of Iraq, northwest of Baghdad).

On October 20, 2006, sixty days into his second deployment, Pearce's five-vehicle convoy was crawling along to its destination, an Iraqi medical center in Mushada, where the soldiers were delivering medical supplies and fresh water. As a field artillery chief surveyor, Pearce sat alone in the hot, glass-enclosed gun turret atop the dusty Humvee—hands on a .50-caliber machine gun—scanning the ground for bombs and the roadside for snipers.

Then it happened. No warning. No one saw it coming. A command-detonated IED buried along the left side of the road exploded under the Humvee that Pearce and his fellow soldiers were riding in. Everything went dark.

A piece of shrapnel the size of a quarter penetrated the right occipital lobe of Pearce's skull and became entangled in his optic nerve. He was clinically dead, but medics

Othello guides Brian through the airport's security checkpoint.

brought him back to life. Once the blast zone was secured, Pearce was med-evaced to a field hospital in Balad, Iraq, where he underwent emergency surgery to remove the shrapnel. In doing so, his optic nerve was damaged, and he lost his vision. Airlifted to Landstuhl, Germany, and then to Bethesda Naval Hospital, and two days later transferred to Walter Reed Army Medical Center's intensive-care unit (at this time, Bethesda and Walter Reed were still separate facilities), Pearce spent forty-seven days in a medically induced coma. "When I started to come out of it, I heard my wife talking to the doctors like a Marine Corps drill sergeant, and I wondered, 'What the heck is my wife doing in Iraq?'"

According to a *Science Daily* article from December 2014 and US Department of Defense statistics, TBIs are among the signature injures impacting veterans serving in Iraq and Afghanistan. Today, like hundreds of thousands of soldiers returning from combat, Pearce, a Purple Heart recipient, struggles with the aftermath of TBI and PTSD, including hearing loss, seizures, sleep disorders, short-term memory loss, flashbacks, nightmares, emotional distance, anxiety, and depression. The simple task of going to the grocery store or the act of hearing a seemingly innocuous sound, such as a soda can hitting the floor, a car backfiring, or a child wailing, can send PTSD-affected veterans into full-blown panic attacks. Like many other veterans, Pearce considered suicide.

Legally blind, Pearce jokes, "I can see enough to get into trouble but not enough to get out of

Guide-Dog Bred

Literally born and bred to be a guide dog, Othello comes from a long line of Labrador Retrievers bred by the Guide Dog Foundation for the Blind, Inc., in Smithtown, New York—a nonprofit organization founded in 1946. The organization began its breeding program in the 1960s, with many of the guide dogs working today being descendants of the original dogs bred by the foundation.

A first-rate ambassador for his breed, Othello embodies the breed's physical and temperamental characteristics—size, gentle disposition, willingness to please, intelligence, trainability—that have fueled its popularity and growth and kept it one of the most popular breeds registered by the American Kennel Club for more than thirty years. The breed's characteristics allow the Labrador Retriever to adapt to many parts of the world and to a variety of work beyond being a hunter's companion, including guide- and service-dog programs, substance-detection work, search and rescue, and more.

trouble." Despite his sense of humor, the road back from the vast Iraqi desert where he nearly lost his life has not been easy for Pearce or his wife and two children. Surviving the explosion was just the beginning of Pearce's journey. Research indicates that when a service member is physically injured or suffers from PTSD, the entire family struggles,

Whether working or relaxing, Othello stays by Brian's side.

too, according to Retired Col. Stephen J. Cozza, MD, associate director of the Center for the Study of Traumatic Stress and a professor of psychiatry at the Uniformed Services University in Bethesda, Maryland. Children are especially vulnerable because they often have a difficult time understanding what is going on with their mom or dad as he or she changes from day to day. Nearly half (48 percent) of all post-9/11 veterans say that they have experienced strains in family relationships since leaving the military, according to a Pew Research Center study from October 2011.

Admittedly, Pearce says he was moody and difficult to get along with at times. "Everyone kept saying, 'You need to get a dog!' But I didn't want one. I was having a hard enough time functioning, being me, being a dad and a husband." Caring for a dog far exceeded his capabilities. Or so he thought.

Often, an important component of therapy for many injured veterans comes from the day-to-day interactions and responsibility of caring for a service dog. Those who are experts say that the seemingly mundane tasks of feeding, walking, exercising, and even petting a dog forces veterans to focus on something—anything—other than themselves. For many veterans suffering from depression, anxiety, panic attacks, and the like, the responsibility associated with canine caregiving saves them from themselves.

At a retreat for military families in 2010, Pearce met with guide-dog representatives and knew immediately that he was ready for a service dog. Teaming with a guide dog was exactly what Pearce needed to regain his confidence, independence, and freedom. The process took about two years. In April 2013, the nonprofit Guide Dog Foundation for the Blind presented the Operation Iraqi Freedom veteran with Othello, a two-year-old black Labrador Retriever, through its America's VetDogs (AVD) project. AVD, also a nonprofit organization, had been formed to serve the needs of disabled veterans from all eras who have honorably served our country.

Pearce believes that God made it a lengthy process because Othello was meant to be his. "The bond was instantaneous," says Pearce. "He has taken to everyone in the family. It's as if he understands that it's his job to take care of the entire family. By taking care of me, he takes care of the entire family, and the family stays together. He seems to understand that everybody needs him."

Trained as both a guide dog and a service dog, Othello takes on full responsibility for Pearce's safety by navigating him through the perils of city traffic as well as the comparative safety of his rural Virginia hometown. Othello enables Pearce to follow a clear path, stopping him for vehicles, crosswalks, and curbs and either leading Pearce away from obstacles or stopping until Pearce can find them. "If I ask him to 'find me a crosswalk,' he'll find one. If I ask him to 'find me an elevator,' he'll find one. It may not be the elevator I want, but it will be the closest elevator."

Othello's training, intelligence, and supreme faithfulness are what keep Pearce from being pitched off a curb into the street or down a flight of stairs. Additionally, as a service dog, Othello helps with Pearce's balance issues and is also trained to interrupt nightmares by falling on Pearce to wake him up.

Although not specifically trained as a PTSD dog (i.e., trained to help mitigate the effects of PTSD in an effort to provide the emotional and physical support a veteran

might need), a strong human–canine relationship has fostered Othello's ability to sense Pearce's elevated anxiety and stress levels. "If we're in public and the crowds or noise are too much," explains Pearce, "Othello quickly figures out that it's not a good place for me. He'll wind himself around my legs until I focus on him. He's very good at redirecting me." Pearce adds, "If we're at a store, I'll say 'outside,' and he takes me to the same door we entered through." Furthermore, Othello helps Pearce remain calm by preventing people from crowding around him or rushing up behind him in public. (Many PTSD dogs are trained to perform a "blocking" behavior, but Othello appears to perform this behavior instinctively as a result of a strong human–canine bond.)

"When I was in law enforcement, I thought the K-9s were the smartest dogs in the world. Then I got Othello. Those cop dogs are nowhere near as smart as Othello," says Pearce, only half jokingly.

It's obvious that Brian and Othello have formed a strong bond.

A loyal companion and the very embodiment of love, Othello shares an exceptional bond with Pearce in a way that most sighted or able-bodied people can never truly understand. A trained guide dog allows veterans like Pearce, as well as all sight-impaired handlers, to regain their confidence, independence, and freedom. No longer are they home-bound or dependent on human guides, such as friends or family. "Othello increased my faith in myself," explains Pearce. "I always knew I could do stuff, but I didn't really want to, and I'm not sure if that's related to PTSD. Othello gives me the confidence to [do] things, including traveling by myself and public speaking."

Othello remains at Pearce's side almost twenty-four hours a day, seven days a week, and he is always eager to serve. The only time Othello stays home is when Pearce enters fishing tournaments. "It's not fair to make him stay on a boat all day, especially in bad weather."

Othello sleeps on or next to Pearce's bed at night. He also rides in the car; goes with Pearce to malls, movie theaters, restaurants, and grocery stores; and attends fundraising and public education events.

Othello's eyes are Pearce's eyes. When navigating with a cane, Pearce was always looking down to see what the cane was bumping into. Today, Othello makes it possible for Pearce to walk while looking up, and that makes him feel like a human being. "Othello has made a huge difference for me. He has boosted my confidence 100 percent. My posture is better, my attitude is better, and I'm able to deal with things much better. It's absolutely phenomenal," Pearce says. "I've regained most of my independence, but not all of it, because blind people still can't drive."

4

THERAPY DOGS IN HISTORY

THERAPY DOGS IN HISTORY

The term *animal-assisted therapy* (AAT) is modern, but the use of animals as companions, healers, and objects of affection has been around since prehistoric times. History is chock full of anecdotes about animals that have therapeutically benefited children and adults. Most likely, these animals—more specifically dogs—received no formal training. Yet, for thousands of years, their innate ability to bond with humans has provided unconditional love, comfort, and a sense of well-being. In their article "An Overview of Animal Facilitated Therapy" in *Iowa State University Veterinarian*, K. L. Boucher and L. A. Will recall one of the earliest documented examples, in ninth-century Gheel, Belgium, in which animals were introduced as part of the therapeutic approach to caring for handicapped individuals.

Plenty of references to the human–animal relationship are scattered throughout early literature, especially when referring to psychiatry, yet the informal introduction of animals for therapeutic benefit appears to have been pioneered by The Retreat, York, England (also referred to as The Retreat York, the Retreat in York, and York Retreat), where animals were plentiful at a home-away-from-home-type facility used to treat the mentally ill and handicapped. Founded in 1796 by wealthy Quaker William Tuke, The Retreat took an unconventional—and most likely informal—approach to treating its patients. A painting dating from 1900 shows an outdoor gathering with four dogs prominently in the foreground and a cat in a tree, suggesting that domesticated animals were very much a part of The Retreat's community.

Dr. Bedford Pierce, The Retreat's medical superintendent from 1892 to 1922, had a beloved black retriever who followed him everywhere, and Dr. Pierce's daughter, Dr. Marjorie Garrod, who was born at The Retreat in 1894, had a parrot that was a favorite of one of the patients. Other dogs belonging to employees, including an Aberdeen Terrier, a Skye Terrier, and a black and tan Collie, lived on the property as well.

With its own farm, The Retreat housed a variety of animals—rabbits, birds, cows, pigs—and anyone walking on the grounds would have encountered these animals. The staff kept horses on the grounds up until World War I, and peacocks lived in the mulberry tree in the ladies' courtyard. A courtyard outside each ward also contained a number of small animals, including rabbits, seagulls, hawks, and various types of poultry, says Dr. Katharine Webb, The Retreat's archivist.

While animals were a fact of life at The Retreat, it's uncertain whether they were deliberately kept specifically for therapy. Regardless, according to Resident Quaker Bronwen Gray, interaction with the animals was thought to reduce outbursts, maintain an overall calmer environment, and uplift and connect patients with a sense of spirituality.

Coal is certified for both search and rescue and therapy work and is part of the "Welcome Home Dogs" group to aid in the demobilization process at Camp Atterbury, Indiana.

The therapeutic benefit of animals did not go unnoticed by the Bethlem Royal Hospital, also in England. Would it be too much to claim that Bethlem had structured animal therapy in place in the mid-1800s? Probably, but evidence of patients' interactions with animals is depicted in an illustration published in 1860 in the *Illustrated London News*. The engraving shows two slightly wary Whippets or small Greyhounds with patients in the men's ward of the hospital while the men play chess, talk, and gaze out windows. At intervals along the tall walls, birdcages are hung, and goldfish bowls sit on high shelves. An illustration from the same time of the women's ward depicts similar fishbowls and birdcages but no dogs.

Although animals were a normal part of life in the hospital, the two dogs shown on the men's ward most likely belonged to the resident physician, Dr. Charles Hood. These animals were thought to possess much power in "raising the sometimes drooping spirits and soothing the troubled minds of the unhappy persons who dwell here," according to former archivist and curator Patricia H. Alleridge in an article she wrote for *Psychiatric Bulletin* in 1991.

Sigmund Freud was another believer in the power of small animals to help residents of psychiatric facilities. Best known as "the father of psychoanalysis," Freud had a constant companion in his beloved Chow Chow, Jofi, who was a frequent fixture in his office even while he engaged in psychotherapy sessions. Freud noticed that Jofi's presence seemed to help patients during their sessions, making them more comfortable and willing to talk more openly. Jofi's body language and mannerisms, Freud believed, were good indicators of the patient's state of mind. Jofi would move away from her normal place next to Freud's desk and lie farther away than usual when a patient was anxious and under stress. For a patient who was depressed, Jofi would lie closer to the couch—close enough so that the patient could reach out his or her hand and touch her, states author Stanley Coren in his book *The Pawprints of History*.

The deliberate introduction of animals into mental hospitals continued into the twentieth century. As early as 1919, dogs were promoted as therapy tools by the US military for psychiatric patients at St. Elizabeth's Hospital in Washington, DC. Later, during World War II, the use of dogs to help veterans recover from war started to take hold.

One story of benevolence involves Lieutenant Colonel William E. King, a chaplain, who used to bring his dog Lulabelle—a mere 6 inches long— with him to the hospital tent while visiting wounded soldiers in Italy. On this particular day, Chaplain King

Nightingale's Observations

Florence Nightingale, who, in the late 1800s, was considered the founder of modern nursing, observed that small pets helped reduce anxiety in children and adults living in psychiatric hospitals.

reached the bed of a young soldier who had lost both of his hands and, according to a nurse, had been unresponsive for days except to reply to questions. When the young soldier saw Lulabelle, he tried to speak.

"What is it, son?" asked Chaplain King.

"Would you let the pup lick my face?" asked the soldier.

Lulabelle scrambled across the soldier's chest, wagging her tail, and licked his face.

"I used to have a dog, sir, and he'd sneak up and lick my face while I was sleeping," he explained. "That's the first time a dog has licked my face since I left home." And then he smiled. Clayton G. Going, author of *Dogs at War*, tells us that when Chaplain King left that day, he left Lulabelle snuggled under the soldier's arm, her head resting on his shoulder.

Lulabelle wasn't the only dog aiding in the recovery of wounded veterans. During World War II, a tiny Yorkshire Terrier is credited with saving the lives of some 250 men and 40 planes. Yet, despite her heroics, the little terrier named Smoky would achieve more enthusiastic praise for her healing effect on wounded soldiers.

Corporal Bill Wynne, at the time a twenty-two-year-old Ohio native, first set eyes on Smoky in March 1944, while he was posted with the US Army Air Corps in Nadzab, New Guinea. A tentmate had found the Yorkie in an abandoned foxhole. Wynne paid two Australian pounds for the underfed, scrawny, half-pint dog, and the two remained inseparable for more than a decade.

When Wynne caught dengue fever and was sent to the 233rd Station Hospital, a friend brought Smoky to visit. Charmed by the tiny dog, the nurses asked if they could bring Smoky around to visit with other patients who had been wounded in the Biak Island invasion.

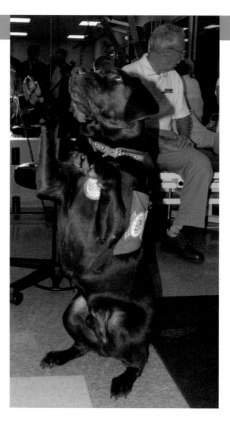

Deuce was the US Army's first therapy dog at Walter Reed Army Medical Center in 2008.

Wynne noticed the powerful effect that Smoky had on the soldiers—how she lightened the mood with her personality and presence. Of course, they also loved the tricks she performed, which Wynne had taught her to relieve the boredom of recuperation.

Word spread, and Wynne and Smoky were invited to perform at a few hospitals in Australia during his convalescence furlough. Men in wheelchairs held Smoky in their arms, and Wynne could see the difference that the 4-pound terrier was making. She made the soldiers smile.

After the war, Wynne, along with Smoky, returned to Cleveland, where the tiny terrier continued therapy-dog work until retiring in 1955.

A documented Department of Defense (DoD) animal-therapy program, in which the American Red Cross began using therapy dogs with wounded soldiers at the Army Air Corps hospital in Pawling, New York, began in 1944. The

Therapy dog Tanner demonstrates obedience by not eating the treats placed on his paws.

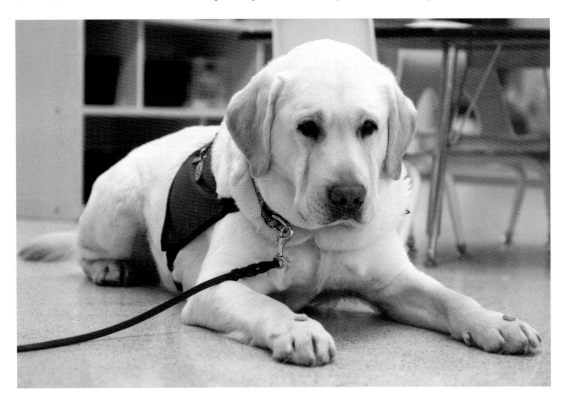

American Red Cross blog goes on to say that "many of the dogs were even acquired as pets for the recovering soldiers." More like a convalescent home than a hospital, the facility encouraged soldiers suffering from "operational fatigue" (most likely what is known as PTSD today) and physical injuries to engage in activities such as horseback riding, fishing, and working at the hospital's "model farm—complete with poultry" according to an article in the June 24, 1944, *Vassar Chronicle*.

Following World War II, a more formal iteration of what would become known as animal-assisted, or pet-assisted, therapy took hold. In the early 1960s, Boris Levinson, a child psychologist at New York's Yeshiva University and a pioneer of animal-assisted therapy, found quite by chance that when his dog Jingles was with him, one of his patients—a very disturbed child—responded better to treatment. Levinson began incorporating Jingles as his "co-therapist" and found that other children who had difficulty communicating seemed more at ease when Jingles was present. In 1962, he published his findings in *Mental Hygiene* in an article entitled "The Dog as Co-Therapist."

It distressed Levinson to find out that many of his colleagues treated his work as a laughing matter. Some jokingly wanting to know what percentage of his fees he paid to the dog. Levinson would go on to write two of the first books on the subject of animal-assisted therapy: *Pet-Oriented Child Psychotherapy* (1969) and *Pets and Human Development* (1973).

Soon, other mental health professionals, including psychiatrists Sam and Elizabeth Corson, who opened the first pet-assisted therapy program at a psychiatric unit at Ohio State University in 1977, were providing solid scientific data that proved the therapeutic value of animals. Among the benefits were reduced stress, improved treatment outcomes, and generally improved mental health.

In the mid-1980s, the military began developing a better understanding of the benefits of the human–canine relationship. When the US Army Surgeon General appointed a human–

animal bond advisor, it set in motion the active pursuit of myriad ways that dogs could be integrated to benefit military personnel. The US Army Veterinary Corps, the DoD Executive Agent for Veterinary Services, took the lead by establishing the US Army Service Dog Training Center (SDTC) at Fort Knox in Kentucky. The program, which ran from 1995 to 2004, was the forerunner for today's puppy prison programs. At that time, select inmates from the Law Enforcement Command's local prison received rehabilitative experience while simultaneously training stray dogs and transforming them into valuable helpers for disabled veterans. Today, puppy prison programs are utilized by many organizations to socialized and train service dogs.

Similar programs have been underway at Walter Reed National Military Medical Center since 2009, when Rick Yount, a licensed social worker, was asked to establish the Warrior Transition Brigade's Wounded Service Dog Program there. The program was designed to help veterans

Therapy dog Lugnut entertains troops recently returned from Afghanistan to Camp Atterbury.

rehabilitating from PTSD and TBIs. While not limited to PTSD- or TBI-affected soldiers, these soldiers seemed to be the best candidates for the program. In addition to spending time with the dogs, which provides increased socialization, confidence, and independence while decreasing emotional detachment and hypervigilance, the soldiers also train the dogs to be service dogs for other veterans.

Around the same time that the Walter Reed program began, a new type of certified therapy dog was being trained to assist soldiers deployed to Iraq and Afghanistan: these dogs made up the first Combat Operational Stress Control (COSC) dog teams. The dogs were attached to COSC units with occupational therapists, with the goal of bringing stress and trauma relief to military personnel in combat zones.

The significant roles played by animals in military conflicts (think cavalry horses, sentry dogs, carrier pigeons, unit mascots, and unofficial battle companions) are well

Animal-assisted therapy is used at many hospitals and medical facilities across the country to lift the spirits of patients.

documented. So, too, are the therapeutic benefits that animals provide. The mere presence of a dog has proved to help soldiers by providing calming and unconditionally loving company and, in many instances, has motivated and encouraged soldiers to seek treatment for PTSDs, TBIs, and physical injuries. Today's specially trained therapy dogs are fulfilling a new role and becoming regular fixtures at military bases both at home and on deployments. (More about these dogs and the work they do in later chapters.)

Long after his death in 1939, and with animal-assisted therapy now recognized as a viable type of treatment for soldiers struggling with PTSD and TBIs, Freud's thoughts remain eerily relevant, as evidenced in letters he wrote to Marie Bonaparte in 1936, referenced in Stanley Coren's *The Pawprints of History*:

Dogs love their friends and bite their enemies, quite unlike people, who are incapable of pure love and always have to mix love and hate in their object relations.

It really explains why one can love an animal like Topsy or Jofi with such an extraordinary intensity; affection without ambivalence, and the simplicity of a life free from the almost unbearable conflicts of civilization, the beauty of an existence complete in itself. And yet despite all divergence in the organic development, there is that feeling of an intimate affinity, of an undisputed solidarity. Often when stroking Jofi, I have caught myself humming a melody which, unmusical as I am, I can't help recognizing as the aria from Don Giovanni:
"A bond of friendship unites us both. . ."

JOEY MIRANDA
&
KATRINA

A ship without Marines is like a garment without buttons.

~ Admiral David D. Porter, USN

Veteran United States Marine Corporal Joseph J. Miranda III spent four years as a member of the field artillery battery responsible for moving, loading, protecting, and maintaining the 155-mm howitzers used by American ground forces. Attached to the 3rd Battalion, 11th Marines, based out of the Marine Corps Air Ground Combat Center, Twentynine Palms, California, Miranda spent time in Okinawa and Tokyo but never deployed to a combat zone. "I had an easy ride compared to some of the guys. I got lucky. I was never deployed," says Miranda, who left the military at the end of his contract in 2002.

That made no difference to Karen Jeffries, a retired naval officer and the founder and president of Veterans Moving Forward, a 501(c)(3) nonprofit organization that trains and provides service dogs at no cost to veterans with physical and mental health challenges (e.g., PTSD, brain injuries, amputation) regardless of whether they sustained their injuries in the military or later, in civilian life.

Joey and Katrina make public appearances to raise awareness about service dogs for veterans.

On February 12, 2007, five years after returning to civilian life, Miranda, a native of Ballston Spa, New York, suffered a severe TBI after falling 38 feet while working with a roofing crew in Albany, New York. He was transported to a local trauma center, and the prognosis was grim; a priest administered last rites. Yet, against all odds, Miranda survived. He underwent six hours of brain surgery, spent seven weeks in a coma, suffered a stroke while in the coma, and eventually endured three months of grueling rehabilitation at Sunnyview Rehabilitation Hospital in Schenectady, New York. Afterward, during a year as an outpatient, he learned how to walk and talk again.

Prior to joining the Marines, Miranda had been enrolled in college, but he admits that he drank too much and didn't study enough. "I wanted something difficult. I wanted a challenge. I wanted something fulfilling," says Miranda. "I liked the Marine Corps' mentality, their toughness." Once a Marine, always a Marine, and, like a true Marine, Miranda remains a fighter. At one point in his rehabilitation, he snapped at his father, "I'll never get to where I want to be by putting (bleeping) pegs in holes. I need to get to the gym."

Miranda's disabilities are different—less conspicuous than, say, those of an amputee or someone confined to a wheelchair. Nonetheless, his ordeal was a tragedy that could break many, and, by all accounts, his recovery has been remarkable. At first glance,

With Katrina, Joey is able to live on his own, drive, and learn new skills.

nothing about Miranda's 6-foot physically fit frame belies a TBI. Yet, he came out of a coma unable to walk, talk, feed himself, or identify any human being, including his parents, and he is now able to live on his own and function successfully in public.

Miranda's recovery is still ongoing. Routine and exercise remain his normalcy. "Coming up with a plan and following through is what helps my TBI," says Miranda. Yet, memory issues persist, and he requires assistance with some aspects of his life, which is what sent Miranda, at the age of thirty-five, and his father, Joseph Miranda, Jr., in search of a service dog.

In the summer of 2013, the elder Miranda applied to Veterans Moving Forward (VMF). After a wait of several months and then an extensive interview process that required several trips to Washington, DC, Miranda was matched in May 2014 with Katrina, an eighteen-month-old yellow Labrador Retriever, bred and donated to VMF by Christina Jones of Pioneer Retriever Kennel in Winchester, Virginia. Their bond was instantaneous, and the two remain inseparable.

Together, Miranda and Katrina have helped raise public awareness about the benefits of service dogs for injured veterans, even participating in a Veterans Moving Forward video that premiered at the annual Cocktails with Canines event in 2014 at the historical and prestigious Army Navy Country Club in Arlington, Virginia. "We want to make a meaningful difference in the lives of our veterans by increasing their safety and independence within their environments," says Jeffries. "We differ from similar services that focus on vets with a singular disability or wartime injuries from a particular war. VMF will help a veteran with health challenges—either mental or physical (or both), and it does not matter to us if he or she lost a leg due to diabetes, a [car] accident, cancer, or injuries."

Miranda's TBI left him with visual agnosia—the inability to recognize objects. While Miranda can still use vision to navigate his environment and pick up objects without trouble, a chicken breast might look like a fish fillet, a cat in the yard might look like a raccoon, and his cell phone might look like a lighter. Prosopagnosia—a form of agnosia—has also left Miranda with the inability to recognize faces, including those of his parents and close friends. A result of damage to a highly specific region of the brain that recognizes faces, Miranda simply passes by friends and family members on the street or in a restaurant, unable to recognize them.

Joey interacts with a fellow veteran's service dog.

Katrina's primary role is to retrieve items that Miranda asks for but can't find or recognize, such as his cell phone, wallet, or keys, which he typically keeps in a basket at his home. When Miranda has trouble recognizing an object, he asks Katrina to retrieve it. His tactile information pathways are intact, so he uses his sense of touch to help recognize the objects that Katrina brings to him. Interestingly, Miranda remains reasonably adept at mastering technical tasks and gadgetry, such as computers, calculators, smart phones, texting, and GPS, yet he struggles with retention problems. The time of day means nothing to him, so Katrina's schedule—eating, walking, pottying, training—helps to keep him grounded and focused.

Because of his agnosia, a huge part of Katrina's training is to recognize the faces of Miranda's parents and close friends. "She knows not to look for attention from people she doesn't know," explains Miranda. "When her vest is on, she's working. People aren't supposed to talk to her. She's connected with me and focused on me. But if we're in the store or a restaurant or walking downtown, and she recognizes my parents or a friend, she'll stop or she'll pull me toward [the person]."

Once a Marine, Always a Marine

Once a person earns the title of "United States Marine," he or she retains it for life. There are no ex-Marines or former Marines. There are active duty Marines, retired Marines, reserve Marines, and Marine veterans.

Joey and Katrina are local celebrities when out and about in their hometown.

For Miranda, the gift of a service dog has changed his life in ways unimaginable to the able-bodied population. Katrina plays an important and ongoing part in his brain-injury recovery by giving him tasks to focus on, such as feeding and caring for her. She enhances his life by giving him more to remember, thereby stimulating his cognitive abilities. The day-to-day interaction and responsibility of caring for a service dog has become an important part of Miranda's therapy in much the same way as service dogs help veterans suffering from PTSD. The seemingly mundane tasks of feeding, walking, exercising, and even petting a dog forces veterans to focus on something—anything—other than themselves. For many veterans suffering from TBIs, depression, anxiety, panic attacks, and so forth, the responsibility associated with canine caregiving saves them from themselves.

In addition to feeding, grooming, and exercising Katrina, part of Miranda's therapy involves keeping up with the day-to-day task of training her, which helps instill brain function. Miranda works regularly with a local trainer to reinforce Katrina's basic obedience skills, such as the *sit*, *down*, and *come* cues, as well as to teach her fun retrieve games, play with her, and just let her be a dog. Teaching Katrina agility commands, including jumping and weave poles, is Miranda's newest challenge. "If Joey's brain is able to reprogram by learning new tasks, by having to learn to read Katrina's body language—to think for her, to get her on a schedule, to get her regular exercise—if these things are helping his brain learn, then he has moved forward and we've met our goals," says Jeffries.

A huge component of caring for a brain-injured person is dependence/independence issues, which eventually take a toll on family members. Miranda's father remains his son's primary caregiver when it comes to some aspects of his life. However, Katrina has enabled Miranda to live independently by giving him a purpose, challenging his abilities, and forcing him to interact and relearn new tasks and behaviors, which, over time, has allowed him to become more independent. "Katrina has given Joey a better living experience. He wouldn't be where he is today without Katrina," says the elder Miranda.

So deep and engrained is the human–canine bond that Katrina recognizes increases in Miranda's respiration and heart rate. She knows when he is anxious, stressed, tired, happy, or sad. During these times, Katrina instinctively calms Miranda to keep him grounded and focused because his agnosia becomes a greater challenge when he is tired or stressed.

Katrina goes well beyond the duties of a service dog, performing traditional yet extraordinary tasks for Miranda. In true service-dog fashion, the 70-pound retriever is Miranda's constant companion. They are together twenty-four hours a day, seven days a week. She accompanies him to the gym six days a week, and they frequently walk into town to Tresa's Café, which has practically become their home away from home. The café is a place where Miranda and Katrina have become the hometown celebrities of Ballston Spa, New York. The waitresses and regular customers are always shouting out, "Hey, Katrina!" as she curls herself at Miranda's feet. The cook exchanges lighthearted banter with Miranda about the daily specials. Miranda's oversized, carefree personality and sense of humor push past his deficiencies and challenges. "I drive, too," he says, "so watch out if you come to upstate New York."

An additional unfortunate consequence of a TBI is the loss of friends. Once social and the life of any party, Miranda now finds that, with the exception of one or two Marine buddies, nearly all of his friends have faded into their own lives. Katrina remains the one constant in his life. His caregiver. His companion. His best friend. "Katrina is the best thing that's happened to me," says Miranda. "The best thing except being born and having great parents."

RACHAEL & JUG

Once you choose hope, anything's possible.

~ Christopher Reeve

I think God must shake His head at me a lot," says Rachael*. "I prayed for guidance because the clear path wasn't enough. And sometimes it's just that easy. Sometimes, when you ask, well, God delivers in a very big, very clear way."

A Gulf War-era veteran, Rachael served four years in the United States Air Force as a nurse stationed at Andrews Air Force Base in Prince George's County, Maryland. Promoted in 2000 to O-3 Captain, Rachael did not deploy, but she sustained a traumatic brain injury (TBI) while on duty. Diagnosed with a concussion, she experienced headaches, dizziness, blurred vision, balance issues, and fatigue. Leaving the military shortly after being promoted, Rachael knew something was wrong but didn't know what. The headaches became progressively and increasingly worse. Struggling with equilibrium problems because of the TBI, she fell several times, sustaining additional concussions.

* Last name has been withheld for privacy.

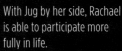

With Jug by her side, Rachael is able to participate more fully in life.

In the fall of 2001, she started law school but left after six months, unable to focus. After moving to Arizona in 2002, Rachael worked as a nurse and then returned to law school in 2005. Again, she had to drop out. "None of it made sense," says Rachael. "I was capable of the work, but I couldn't focus. I couldn't think properly. I didn't know what was wrong."

The debilitating headaches, dizziness, ongoing balance problems, nausea, sensitivity to light, and fatigue continued to worsen. Unable to maintain employment due to her service-related disabilities, in 2009, she was deemed "individual unemployable," or what is known as IU by the VA. Diagnosed with status migrainosus—a condition in which a migraine lasts longer than seventy-two hours and may require hospitalization to treat the pain and dehydration from vomiting—Rachael was unable to work or attend school. "I wanted to work," says Rachael. "I went to ten different places, asking for work. They all said no because of the headaches. It's a very humbling experience to ask for work and get turned down."

Their extraordinary bond means that Jug is in sync with Rachael's needs and symptoms.

For years, Rachael avoided the label *disabled*, wanting only to be normal. Rachael's disability is less obvious than, say, that of a person in a wheelchair or an amputee, and, unless she is having a "stormy" day, little about her appearance belies a disability. Nonetheless, she struggles daily. Once able to run five miles a day, five days a week, she now has days when she can't climb the stairs in her home.

Even worse are the days when her mind simply isn't the same. When the pain clouds her brain and she forgets names, dates, and recent conversations. Some days, the thoughts come back with prompting—with "mental sticky notes" that she creates in her mind. Most days, however, she simply adjusts, as she has learned to do. "For a woman who identifies herself largely by her mental capacity," says Rachael, "this shift in capability is no small thing."

Despite medications, the unrelenting, debilitating symptoms continued. Some days, opening her eyes in a lighted room could bring on stabbing pain. Subsequently, she has had times when she's spent five or six days at a time, twenty-four hours a day, in a darkened room. A nerve block procedure designed to decrease the symptoms only made them worse, sending the migraines out of control.

In early 2014, at the urging of a friend, Rachael went in search of a service dog. "I had never thought of a service dog," she says. "I had no idea what a service dog could do for me."

Eight months after applying to Veterans Moving Forward (VMF), who provides service dogs at no cost to veterans with physical and mental health challenges regardless of whether they sustained their injury in the military or later in civilian life, Rachael received the call that would change her life for the better. Karen Jeffries, president and founder of VMF, called to tell her that they had a dog for her.

Jug, a two-year-old, 65-pound yellow Labrador Retriever named in memory of Major Andrew "Jug" Turner, a Tuskegee Airman and commander of the 100th Fighter Squadron, 332nd Fighter Group, 15th Air Force, US Army Air Corps, is trained to assist Rachael with balance and stability issues to prevent falling while walking or navigating up and down stairs and to help "brace" her while she repositions herself, such as when getting up or down. Jug is also trained to search, find, and retrieve on command her bag of medications from anywhere in the house, which also includes opening a drawer, if necessary. Because of balance issues related to her TBI, and because bending over may cause her to fall, Jug is trained to retrieve Rachael's cell phone, car keys, cane, and anything else she might drop.

Although not specifically trained to interrupt nightmares or alert Rachael to an impending migraine, Jug performs these behaviors on his own—innate behaviors, say experts, as a result of a deep emotional human–canine bond with Rachael. "The first week he came to live with me, he woke me up in the middle of the night. He had

my bag of medications in his mouth," says Rachael. "I didn't know what he wanted, so I sent him back to his bed, which is about 3 feet from my bed. About an hour later, he woke me up again, and again I sent him back to his bed. I thought he was bored and wanted to play. An hour later, I woke up with a horrible migraine. Had I paid attention the first time, I would not have been as sick. I don't know how, but somehow he could predict that I was going to

Jug helps ease the physical and emotional effects of Rachael's disability.

have a migraine three hours before it happened."

Most trainers agree that dogs can't be trained to detect a migraine (or seizure) in advance; rather, dogs pick up on their owners' signals. The preheadache or premonitory phase of a migraine is the migraineur's "yellow light"—a warning that a migraine is coming. Common symptoms include, but are not limited to, concentration problems, difficulty speaking, fatigue, hyperactivity or hypoactivity, increased thirst, repetitive yawning, and sleep issues, which can occur as early as twenty-four hours before any head pain. Humans may not realize that they are sending out signals, yet experts believe that dogs, who are experts at reading body language, pick up on the cues before the headaches occur.

Jug alerts Rachael in advance of a migraine by first pawing at her leg. If she fails to pay attention, he will lay his head on her lap. If she continues to ignore him, he will back up and bark at her. He will also retrieve her bag of medications, without being commanded to do so, and drop it in her lap. It's as if he's telling her, "Take your meds! Take your meds!" He is 100-percent spot-on at alerting her to impending migraines, according to Rachael, now that she realizes what his alerting behavior means.

Research suggests that alerting behavior is not breed-, age-, or gender-specific; rather, according to John J. Ensminger's book *Service and Therapy Dogs in American Society,* the effectiveness of an alerting dog "depends greatly upon the human companion to recognize and respond appropriately to the dog's alerting behavior." Today, Rachael is more attuned to Jug's alerts, which allows her to take her medication ahead of time, thereby warding off a severe migraine episode.

Before Jug came to live with Rachael—while he was still with his foster family—Jeffries gave him a T-shirt belonging to Rachael. For months and months, Jug slept with the T-shirt, absorbing and becoming familiar with her scent. When Rachael and Jug first met, he immediately recognized her scent, which may help to explain why he was able to alert to her within the first week.

"When I'm having a really bad migraine and there's nothing Jug can do to make it better," says Rachael, "he carries around that same T-shirt. It's like a comfort blanket to him. He's very sensitive, and it bothers him when he can't 'fix' me." Perhaps this is a testament to the Labrador Retriever's long history as hardy retrievers with gentle, friendly dispositions.

"Jug and his beautiful brain are an amazing gift, but, in all honesty, he is a gift that I had a terrible time accepting," says Rachael. Meeting with the veteran–canine selection committee of VMF in October 2014, Rachel shied away from what they had to say. "Even with all of my education and experience, I had never put together that my injuries and symptoms totaled a TBI. How could my injury be the same as someone who'd had their Humvee blown up in Iraq? It didn't seem possible. But it was, and it is. And still I struggled."

In a serendipitous twist, Jug's foster family was a retired diplomat and his wife, who live in Vienna, Virginia, yet they had met more than fifty years prior while freshmen at Washington High School in Phoenix—the same high school where Rachael had worked as a nurse when she moved to the Sonoran Desert in 2002.

"God spoke. I heard. Jug came home with me," says Rachael. "I am a different person than I was fifteen years ago. I have a disability that I am learning to both live with and talk about. God provided Jug as a tool to do both. I don't know where I would be without him. I'm not going to spend the rest of my life—24/7—in a darkened room. I still have bad days, but Jug gives me something to get up for—even when my head is pounding."

Quotes from Rachael's blog (www.the unexpected life.net) used with permission.

5

COMBAT AND OPERATIONAL STRESS-CONTROL DOGS

COMBAT AND OPERATIONAL STRESS-CONTROL DOGS

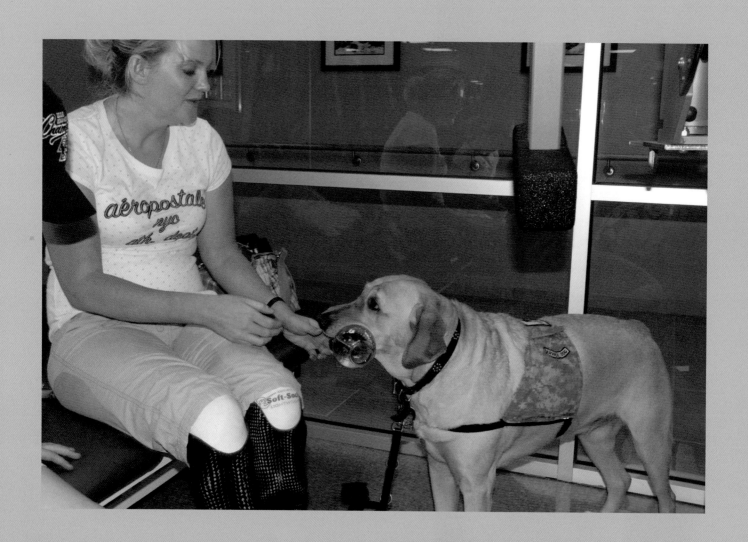

W

hen paperwork landed on Maj. General Gale
Pollock's desk requesting the deployment of two dogs to Iraq,
the first woman to serve as Acting Surgeon General of the US
Army did not need convincing. Pollock anticipated that the
dogs would safeguard the behavioral health of deployed
soldiers by providing an element of stress relief.

Boe and Budge, Zeke and Albert, Butch and Zach, and
Apollo and Timmy represented a new category of military
working dogs—specially trained and skilled therapy dogs.
Between 2007 and 2011, these eight dogs would make up
the first Combat and Operational Stress-Control (COSC)
dog therapy response team.

The concept is so simple, so rooted in the history and
narrative of the human–canine bond, that it's challenging
to believe that the idea wasn't conceived years ago. The idea
to deploy COSC dogs evolved at the Walter Reed National
Military Medical Center. Those caring for wounded soldiers
began to notice that George, a Golden Retriever trained
to help patients adjust to their new prosthetic limbs, was
also providing emotional support to the wounded soldiers,
according to a 2012 article by William Krol titled "Training
the Combat and Operational Stress Control Dog: An
Innovative Modality for Behavioral Health."

Why not deploy specially trained therapy dogs with the COSC teams' occupational therapists to help soldiers struggling with the trauma of combat? To help break down the stigma attached to mental healthcare?

History is chock full of informal anecdotes and documented evidence of the use of animals—especially dogs—in military conflicts around the world. Also documented is the therapeutic use of dogs to help soldiers, as well as civilians, recover from emotional and physical trauma. Pollock had firsthand knowledge of the benefits that therapy dogs provided to soldiers struggling with PTSD—soldiers who, in some cases, would not speak to people but would talk to the therapy dogs. If therapy dogs could get combat soldiers talking about their experiences—their trauma—she felt that the soldiers would be better off in the long run.

Within days of stepping into position as Acting Surgeon General, says Pollock, she found the request to deploy therapy dogs on her desk. She gave permission for the project, and her health team executed it.

All of the dogs chosen for COSC work were Labrador Retrievers; pictured here are Boe and Budge.

The army partnered with America's VetDogs (AVD) and developed a pioneering program that would provide specially trained therapy dogs to soldiers during their deployment as part of Operation Iraqi Freedom (OIF) and Operation Enduring Freedom (OEF). AVD searched its database of available dogs, which are selectively bred by its sister organization, the Guide Dog Foundation for the Blind. Before these dogs set foot in Iraq or Afghanistan, they would need to undergo in-depth predeployment training—similar to, but not as rigorous as, that of their canine counterparts who are trained to search for buried mines and artillery, sniff out IEDs, or track down the people who stashed the explosives.

No matter how healthy or good-looking the dogs are, if they are fearful, shy, or reactive, then they won't fare well downrange. Their main duties involve calming and providing stress relief and comfort to soldiers—not making them more anxious. Therefore, only dogs of the highest quality with stable, sound—nearly perfect—temperaments and nerves of steel were considered. The dogs needed to be confident, comfortable, and adaptable in new and stressful situations, including responding reliably to multiple handlers and assuming different roles in their therapy work.

While COSC dogs were a new idea, dogs have been part of the military for years. US Army Spc. Kory Wiels and his military working canine Cooper take a break after searching a house for weapons and homemade explosives in Arab Jabour, Iraq.

Gunfire, mortar blasts, and IED explosions are part of the landscape that COSC dogs and soldiers face daily in the war-ravaged countries of Iraq and Afghanistan. Therefore, the dogs needed to be exposed and conditioned to these occurrences, as well as to all of the elements that they were likely to encounter once deployed, including weather conditions, terrain, and the sights, sounds, and smells of military vehicles, aircraft, and Black Hawk helicopters. Even dogs with plenty of strength and stamina can struggle when deployed to foreign settings, so the chosen canines needed plenty of energy to engage in physical training exercises yet possess an "off switch" so they could lie quietly while in clinical situations. Environmental conditions and the availability of veterinarians would be unpredictable once deployed; therefore, these dogs needed to pass a thorough veterinary check and receive a clean bill of health, too.

AVD selected candidates from a pool of about twenty dogs, which they narrowed down to twelve dogs and then to the final eight Labrador Retrievers. Although plenty of breeds, including mixed breeds, fit the bill for therapy dogs, Labrador Retrievers are known for their intelligence, trainability, devotion, sensitivity, happy demeanor, and eagerness to please. They are seen as friendly, lovable dogs, and they don't have the aggressive reputation that many military-trained dogs do. And, as any Lab owner will attest, Labs are more likely to pester, snuggle, and lick you to death, and those aren't bad traits for a therapy dog.

Training COSC dogs and acclimating them to this newly developed, innovative, and demanding job would prove to be a six-month process. During training at AVD's Long Island, New York, campus as well as at army bases and fire stations, trainers reinforced the dogs obedience training, basic commands, and controllability. They monitored each dog's reactions when exposed to

Command Sgt. Maj. Ronnie Kelley, US Army Central, pets Maj. Eden, Task Force 31, 98th Combat Stress Control Detachment's military therapy dog, while visiting Afghanistan in July 2014.

Hudson, a therapy dog, gets fitted for his goggles by Capt. Christine Beck, 528th Combat Operational Stress Control Unit, during predeployment training.

different types of vehicles, sights, and noises, including flashing lights and horns. Dogs were trained to jump in and out of stationary helicopters and were exposed to the sounds of gunfire, ranging from automatic weapons to pistols. Fearful dogs were dropped from the COSC program, but trainers worked further with those displaying only mild anxiety.

Dogs, including plenty of Labrador Retrievers, can be scavengers by nature, which could be problematic once deployed, so the canines also were taught to ignore food distractions.

The weather conditions in Afghanistan and Iraq are intense and unforgiving. For that reason, dogs were conditioned to wear and were deployed with protective gear, such as special earmuffs for noise protection and goggles to safeguard their eyes from blowing sand. Special canine boots protected their paws from the hot ground, and cooling jackets were standard gear for days when the mercury consistently soared above 120 degrees Fahrenheit (48.8 degrees Celsius). Afghanistan winters also can be harsh, so warm vests protected dogs from subarctic conditions. Dogs also wore special packs to carry their own food and supplies so they wouldn't add to the loads of the soldiers caring for them.

The primary handlers for the COSC dogs were occupational therapists, and, they, too, underwent specialized predeployment training to learn basic canine handling techniques. These men and women did not necessarily come from dog backgrounds, and none of them had previously trained a dog or utilized animal-assisted therapy. In addition to the occupational therapists' duties as officers-in-charge, educators, and mental health officers, they had the added responsibility and stress of caring for highly trained and valuable military dogs while deployed in a combat zone. A deployed environment is much, much different than a fenced backyard, and when deployed 8,000 miles from home, these dogs are absolutely dependent on their handlers for everything.

For those handlers with no dog-ownership or training experience, the learning curve proved steep. But, by the time they finished the five days of training, they were well-versed in general veterinary care, such as how to recognize injuries, canine stress, and heat casualties. They had received plenty of hands-on training and had learned basic obedience skills and proper handling and praising techniques. Genuine, heartfelt praise is essential in the human–canine relationship, especially with working dogs, and it frequently proves a difficult concept for many trainers to master.

To practice and reinforce their training, dogs and their primary and secondary handlers trained in a variety of safe and controlled military environments, including the post exchange, hospital, and mental health clinics, as well as the gun range and motor pool. Most importantly, they had to learn how to utilize the dogs downrange—how to break down barriers.

In December 2007, traveling on official army orders, Sgt.1st Class Boe and Sgt.1st Class Budge were deployed to Iraq with the 85th Medical

Budge and Boe were the first COSC dogs deployed.

COSC dog Major Timmy greets service members at Bagram Air Field, Afghanistan.

Detachment as the first COSC dogs trained to provide soldiers with emotional support in a war zone. SFC Boe and SFC Budge were first-rate ambassadors for the breed, embodying the Labrador Retriever's desirable characteristics of gentle disposition, sweet temperament, willingness to please, intelligence, and trainability. These are traits that have been selectively bred for generations, helping to fuel the breed's popularity and growth and keeping the Labrador Retriever as one of the most popular breeds registered by the American Kennel Club (AKC). These same traits have allowed the Labrador Retriever to adapt to many parts of the world and to a variety of work beyond the shooting field—most notably as military, law-enforcement, guide, and service dogs.

Seventeen months later, in May 2009, SFC Zeke and SFC Albert deployed to Iraq, with Maj. Timmy and Maj. Apollo deploying to Afghanistan the following year. Maj. Butch would follow his canine counterparts, deploying to Iraq in February 2011.

As part of the Army's COSC prevention team, the dogs traveled with their handlers between forward operating bases (FOBs) and patrol bases (PBs), safeguarding the behavioral health of soldiers in the combat zone. While COSC dogs are not saving soldiers' lives by sniffing out buried mines and pressure-plate IEDs like their explosive-detecting canine counterparts, SFC Boe and SFC Budge, as well as the other dogs, were able to do what humans could not—provide stress relief and get the soldiers talking, which, in the long run, helped to save the lives of countless soldiers who struggled with PTSD and teetered on the brink of suicide.

Why dogs have the ability to connect so deeply with people remains a bit of a mystery. In his book *Man Meets Dog*, Austrian ethologist Konrad Lorenz explored the different types of human–dog relationships. Lorenz believed that strong human–canine bonds were created when both human and dog "resonated"—when they were fully in sync with each other.

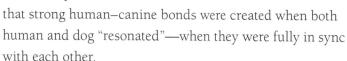

Timmy shared positive vibes with not only the troops but also with the locals of Jalalabad.

How is it possible that dogs have the uncanny ability to sense when things are amiss in a person's life? How can dogs elicit positive responses from people struggling with emotional issues, including PTSD, when the best efforts of family members and trained professionals have failed? And why do humans invite and relish close relationships and communication with dogs? Surely a dog's love for humans—and vice versa—has to be based on more than treats, tennis balls, and belly rubs.

Oxytocin and dopamine may in part decode the strong feelings of attachment that people have for dogs. We know from previous research that oxytocin, the "feel-good" hormone produced in the brain and associated with nurturing and attachment, spikes in a person's body—causing some owners to feel warm and overwhelmed with loving feelings—when they pet a dog or gaze into a dog's eyes.

A 2015 study by Japanese researchers at Azabu University in Sagamihara took this theory one step further by measuring oxytocin levels in the urine of thirty dogs and owners before and after they interacted for thirty minutes. Researcher Takefumi Kikusui's primary findings were that oxytocin increased in people and dogs who engaged in "long gazes" (defined as 100 seconds in the first five minutes of the encounter) with one another and showed high levels of stroking and petting. However, oxytocin levels did not increase in owners and dogs who were in the "short gaze" category, nor did the levels increase in pairs of owners and hand-raised wolves. Compared with dogs, the wolves scarcely gazed at their owners, and their oxytocin levels barely budged.

Of the dogs and owners who spent the greatest amount of time looking into each other's eyes, both male and female dogs experienced a 130-percent rise in oxytocin levels, and both male and female owners experienced a 300-percent increase, reported David Grimm in his April 16, 2015,

Butch deployed to Iraq in February 2011.

article for *Science Magazine* titled "How Dogs Stole Our Hearts." The duration of gazing—not touching—appeared to be the factor that spiked increases in oxytocin. Mutual gazing, as it's sometimes called, and oxytocin levels appear to exist in a continuous or positive loop in which gazing increases oxytocin and oxytocin increases gazing, which, in turn, increases the likelihood of the owner's talking to and touching his or her dog, thereby contributing to and strengthening the human–canine bond.

Several years ago, researchers from the School of Psychology, Interdisciplinary Center (IDC) in Herzliya, Israel, and the Department of Psychology at the University of California, Davis, looked at pet ownership and the human–canine bond through the perspective of attachment theory. With early roots in ethological studies conducted by Lorenz in the 1930s, attachment theory was defined in 1969 by John Bowlby, a British psychologist, psychiatrist, and psychoanalyst, as a "lasting psychological connectedness between two living beings" in his book *Attachment: Attachment and Loss, Volume 1.*

In a nutshell, attachment theory originally was used to

While the dogs trained with specific handlers, they bonded with all of the soldiers.

conceptualize child–parent relationships, with the main notion being that an infant needs a primary caregiver who is available and responsive to his or her needs without being overbearing. Mothers, for instance, who are devoted and available to their babies and responsive to their needs instill a feeling of security in their kids.

Based on their study, the results of which were published in 2011, in the *Journal of Research in Personality*, Sigal Zilcha-Mano and his colleagues believe that when a person's relationship with a pet involves tenderness, warmth, stability, and loyalty, it can lead to feelings of being unconditionally loved and accepted. Feelings of complete acceptance may, in turn, cause people to turn to their pets for comfort and reassurance during difficult times.

Therapy dogs have the mysterious ability to sense which soldiers need them the most, which soldiers are having a bad day, and which soldiers are feeling sad or depressed. The dogs also know that they can make the soldiers feel better by

The dogs provided vital therapy just by being dogs. Pictured is COSC dog Zack.

hanging out with them. By simply playing, fetching, getting petted, or, in many instances, providing a sympathetic, nonjudgmental ear, COSC dogs became powerful tools for combat soldiers—the soldiers' number-one morale boosters. Who better to spill your problems to than a dog, especially when you're in what may arguably be one of the worst places in the world?

The dogs broke the ice with soldiers and provided comfort, reassurance, and a sense of unconditional love to those battling a less visible enemy: stress. Just by being himself, a COSC dog has the innate ability to make a positive difference in how the soldier's day—or even the rest of his or her deployment—would go. For whatever reasons, the dogs were able to get the soldiers to open up about their trauma, thus accomplishing exactly what Maj. General Pollock had hoped for when she approved the request of the 85th Medical Detachment (COSC) in 2007.

Studies are underway to understand exactly how the dogs are helping soldiers. In spite of scientific research and analysis, could the human–canine relationship be as simple as not having to explain yourself or talk about your feelings if you don't want to, as reflected by retired Green Beret Brian Anderson. Perhaps this simplicity helps explain why many people routinely turn to dogs for the unconditional joy, love, comfort, and calmness that other humans often fail to provide.

Taking Care of COSC Dogs

Safeguarding the physical and mental health of COSC dogs, as well as all military dogs, is paramount. Upon their return home, COSC dogs return to the AVD campus, where they are evaluated by trainers. By comparing the dogs' predeployment and postdeployment behaviors, trainers are better able to gauge and identify potential temperament and behavioral problems, including canine PTSD. Dogs receiving a clean bill of health are retrained and given their next Army assignment.

According to Valerie Cramer, guide- and service-dog trainer at AVD and trainer of the COSC dogs and handlers, retraining often involved reinforcing basic obedience commands, such as *sit, down, walk back*, and so forth, that had fallen by the wayside while deployed. Other behaviors, such as snatching food off tables and counters, that might have been acceptable in the theater but undesirable in a hospital or other medical reassignment, needed to be addressed as well.

COSC dog Sgt. 1st Class Boe sits in the 1st Brigade Combat Team, 101st Airborne Division Operations Center.

Despite their rock-solid, nearly perfect temperaments and stellar training, therapy dogs are still *Canis lupus familiaris*—dogs. Both genetic and environmental influences impact the development of canine behavior. Deploying to a combat zone requires dogs to adapt and acclimate to varying environments, new sights, sounds, people, and, sometimes, new handlers. How they react depends a lot on their genetic predispositions, not just their training.

In 2009, SFC Boe and SFC Budge rotated home and awaited their next assignment. SFC Zeke and SFC Albert were trained to take their place. Inherently, Zeke and Albert—like Boe and Budge—knew when they were at work versus when they could relax. Friendly and well-mannered, they thrived on interaction, yet SFC Albert would get overly excited in unfamiliar situations. On the other hand, SFC Zeke responded more timidly, and he tested his boundaries when he was transferred to a new handler in 2010. With his previous handler remaining at the forward operating base, Zeke was confused and didn't know from whom to accept commands. One trainer likened him to a child with a substitute teacher, wanting to see what he could get away with. A week or so later, in true Labrador Retriever sensibility and professionalism, he adapted to his new handler and was back to fulfilling his duties as a therapy dog. Major Lori Filke, Captain Cecilia Najera, and Captain

David Dougherty wrote about these experiences in an article titled "Occupational Therapists as Dog Handlers: The Collective Experience with Animal-Assisted Therapy in Iraq" for the April–June 2012 issue of the *United States Army Medical Department Journal*.

Diane Sawyer reported on ABC World News Report that there are roughly 2,500 dogs trained for military service, but less than

While many dogs, like Rosco, are trained to help veterans affected by PTSD, it is debated whether military dogs can also exhibit symptoms.

a dozen specially skilled COSC dogs were deployed into combat zones to provide emotional support. Moving the dogs was a huge undertaking. As a result, once the dogs deployed downrange, they tended to stay downrange. Transporting the dogs and all of their gear—crates, backpacks, food, toys, long lines, leashes, medications—by helicopter or airplane was challenging. An even bigger deal was getting the dogs on the manifest so they could ride up top with the soldiers, rather than below in a crate. Many of the soldiers were so appreciative of the dogs that they gladly gave up their space on the aircraft to make the dogs comfortable.

Unlike many of today's companion dogs who no longer have full-time (or even part-time) jobs as their ancestors did, COSC dogs, as well as all military dogs, do have a job, a purpose. Granted, their work conditions are unconventional and usually stressful, and with that job comes multiple handlers and deployments. Because of the dogs' high demand

and relatively low numbers compared to their handlers (the military has between eight and fourteen potential handlers for every two dogs deployed), wrote William Krol in his aforementioned article, the dogs seldom get R&R between deployments (although they do get daily down time).

Working dogs who remain in good health are often deployed multiple times, sometimes even seeing back-to-back deployments, as was the case with SFC Boe. For nearly fifteen of the eighteen months during which SFC Boe was deployed, Captain Cecilia Najera was her handler. Toward the end of Boe's tour, Najera began noticing changes in the dog's behavior. When soldiers approached her, she often turned away. "It was as if," Najera says, "she had absorbed too much sadness," wrote Rebecca Frankel in her 2014 book *War Dogs: Tales of Canine Heroism, History, and Love.*

Likewise, Timmy, who was easy to handle and loved being petted, touched, cuddled, and kissed, as well as riding in the helicopter, enjoyed one day a week of R&R. At the end, he would still work when asked to do so (after all, he's a Labrador Retriever!), but after three tours and roughly thirty-eight months of deployment, he eventually grew tired of the head petting.

Whether or not dogs suffer from PTSD is a hotly debated topic. Canine PTSD is not a fully recognized veterinary behavioral phenomenon, but empirical data suggest that it exists, and it's probably more common that people believe. Given what we know about the intricacies of the canine brain, it stands to reason that dogs—despite their training and conditioning—are not immune to the fallout of stressful, chaotic environments. How would it be possible for therapy dogs (or any military or law-enforcement dog) to continually absorb the stress, anxiety, anger, rage, and sadness of soldiers on a daily basis and walk away emotionally unscathed?

Returning home, SFC Albert was reassigned to Fort Gordon's Warrior Transition Battalion, where he continues to work. SFC Boe and SFC Budge were reassigned to serve at Eisenhower Army Medical Center (EAMC) at Fort Gordon, Georgia. In 2010, SFC Budge was diagnosed with lymphoma and passed away. SFC Boe is now retired, as are SFC Zeke, who did three tours, and Maj. Timmy, Master Sgt. Apollo, and Maj. Butch, who each did two tours. Maj. Zack developed a blood disease and passed away.

No COSC dogs are currently being trained for deployment, yet the work they did remains vivid in the hearts of the soldiers they touched. Not long ago, a veteran called Cramer and told her that seeing a COSC dog while deployed changed his whole outlook. "I hear stories about what these dogs did for soldiers, and I'm honored to have been a part of it," says Cramer. "The dogs were so beneficial in boosting morale and making the soldiers' lives better—even if for only a brief time during the day."

PAUL UTTER
&
ELLIE

Aim High . . . Fly, Fight, Win.

~ US Air Force motto

Thirty years after leaving the United States Air Force, Paul Utter is finally able to deal with the long-term effects of PTSD—thanks to Ellie, a Golden Retriever donated by Southeastern Guide Dogs' Paws for Patriots program.

As a military policeman, and later as a ground-safety noncommissioned officer (NCO), Utter investigated military accidents such as auto or plane crashes, fires, gunshot wounds, and so forth. Utter also worked with troops returning from the war and patrolled the Berlin Wall by helicopter. After only two weeks on the job, Utter responded to a sniper incident in which a young airman had lost his life. That incident remains one of the biggest PTSD triggers for Utter.

During his eight years in uniform, as well as four years in the New York Air National Guard, he saw more than his share of horrific tragedies, experiences that left him struggling with the invisible wounds of PTSD, including claustrophobia, fear of crowds, panic attacks, anxiety, stress, and flashbacks.

Paul feels comfortable and confident with Ellie by his side.

Back in the Vietnam era, PTSD wasn't as widely recognized as it is today. According to Robert Poole in his September 2010 article for Smithsonian.com titled "The Pathway Home Makes Inroads in Treating PTSD," the "stress-related illness" was called "post-Vietnam syndrome."

The dynamics of the Vietnam War were also different, and the moral revulsion of the public toward the war did not bode well for soldiers returning stateside in the 1970s. As a result, many veterans preferred to remain silent about their troubles. And while treatment options for PTSD have come a long way since 1981, the year that Utter left the military, nearly thirty years would pass before Utter found a measure of peace, independence, and freedom from PTSD in the form of a service dog.

The Research Triangle Institute concludes that 830,000 Vietnam veterans have full-blown or partial PTSD, but only 55,119 have filed claims. Equally important, research indicates that soldiers need not experience combat in order to suffer from PTSD.

Utter may have left the military, but the battles inside him continued for years. Before Ellie, Utter was held captive by the recurring images and nightmares of his experiences from all those years ago. He isolated himself and avoided going out in public, especially to crowded areas like malls, movies, restaurants, and the like. He drank too much, and, like many veterans, he contemplated suicide.

Burying those images the best he could, he went on with his life. He married, raised his children, and spent five years working as a drug and alcohol counselor for a private hospital in New York and then fifteen years for the New York State Department of Corrections.

When Utter's father passed away in 1996, it "shook loose" something, dredging up hidden memories, and images of the past came crashing back in. "I remember sitting in a chair when a black and white silhouette passed by," says Utter. "It was a partial scene from my military service. It was like a motion picture, very quick. I thought, 'What just happened?'"

Moving to Palmetto, Florida, in 2008, Utter found himself less than a mile from the Southeastern Guide Dogs campus. He began volunteering—first walking the dogs every day, then transporting them to veterinary appointments, and then helping with puppy socialization. "I connected with the dogs," says Utter. "It was just me and the dogs. A safe place, away from crowds."

Paul winds up to throw the first pitch at Tropicana Field.

Around the same time, a counselor from the local VA asked Utter, "Why don't you get a PTSD dog?" Utter was matched with Ellie in 2011, a one-and-a-half-year-old Golden Retriever trained by Southeastern Guide Dogs and donated through their Paws for Patriots program, which is designed to provide dogs to veterans living with PTSD.

A "career change" dog, Ellie had been donated by a breeder in Nevada. Unfortunately, a diagnosis of mild hip dysplasia at one year of age precluded her from future work as a breeding or guide dog. Yet, Ellie embodied all of the breed's outstanding characteristics—a quiet, intelligent, quickly responsive, and biddable temperament, as well as a generous spirit, high level of sociability toward people, and willingness to learn and retain whatever she is taught, which makes her the perfect service-dog candidate for the organization's veterans' dog program. An instantaneous bond formed, and Utter and Ellie have been inseparable since day one.

"I can't tell you the difference this dog is making," says Utter. "She gives me safety, confidence. She is able to detect or bring me out of a flashback faster than any human. She gives me comfort. It's like she takes you out of yourself. I don't know where I'd be without her right now."

Specifically trained to mitigate the symptoms of PTSD, Ellie is trained to perform twenty-six commands, from basic obedience to PTSD commands, among them hug, block, watch, and check, among others.

"Personal space is very important to people with PTSD," explains Utter. "Most people aren't aware of another person's personal space, but people with PTSD are acutely aware of it."

As a PTSD-trained dog, Ellie "blocks" people from getting too close by providing a buffer or barrier between Utter and other people. Simply put, she keeps people at a distance, and she'll stay in the blocking position until Utter tells her to do otherwise. Ellie also will "watch," which is similar to blocking except that she moves in front of Utter from his left side across to his right side to "watch his back." "She becomes eyes in the back of my head," says Utter. "She'll alert to anything that isn't right."

Like most service dogs, Ellie is hardwired to Utter's emotions through an impenetrable human–canine bond. She knows his moods—when he is happy, sad, anxious, stressed, and so forth—and can sense elevations in his heart rate and respiration. She's trained to "hug"—put her front feet on his lap or shoulders, thereby putting her face close to his. She'll lick his face or do whatever is necessary to get his attention. Turning his attention to Ellie calms Utter by slowing his heart rate before he goes into a full-blown panic attack or meltdown. On those occasions when Utter does experience a major anxiety attack—a state he describes as not being passed out but not in the present, either— Ellie will stretch out beside him and place her face next to his, bringing him back to the present faster than any medications or humans have been able to do.

Paul and Ellie at a Tampa Bay Rays game.

Utter relies on Ellie to gauge the safety of his surroundings, which allows him to venture out in public without having to be constantly hypervigilant. Seemingly mundane everyday activities, like grocery shopping or walking through a crowded shopping mall, are anything but routine for veterans suffering from PTSD. For example, a grocery-store aisle may represent a threat for a person struggling with PTSD, causing him or her to put all senses on red alert. The "dead space"—the space you can't see between the aisles—may trigger a flashback, taking the person back to the jungles of Vietnam or to a crowded, chaotic alley in Iraq or Afghanistan. The seemingly innocuous sound of the clashing of shopping carts or a can of beans hitting the floor may trigger fears of an imminent explosion or flashbacks of a firefight or a deadly IED ready to blow apart life and limb. A person passing by with a shopping cart may be a suicide bomber. A well-hidden sniper may be lurking just around the corner. Veterans struggling with PTSD always feel under attack when in crowded areas, which explains why so many veterans avoid public venues.

For Utter, these experiences are real. So real that Ellie is trained to "check" each aisle. She will go ahead of Utter (on leash) to the end of the aisle, look left, look right, and alert to anyone in either direction. If her tail and head go up and her back goes straight, Utter knows that someone is there. Thus, when he goes around the corner, he's not startled or surprised because Ellie has alerted him to the person's presence. That person may be another shopper, a sales clerk, or a vendor; regardless, it's the only way that Utter can get down the aisle and around the corner without experiencing anxiety, stress, elevated heart rate and blood pressure, and possibly a full-blown anxiety attack.

True to her breed's characteristics, Ellie loves to work and play. She accompanies Utter everywhere, including to Tropicana Field in St. Petersburg, Florida, where he threw out the first pitch at a Tampa Bay Rays game in May 2013. Today, Utter pays it forward by helping others. He speaks on behalf of Southeastern Guide Dogs to raise public awareness about the benefits of service dogs for veterans. Additionally, he has sponsored two puppies, and Governor Rick Scott recently awarded Utter the Volunteer Florida Champion of Service Award for his service to Southeastern Guide Dogs.

Ellie has drawn out Utter's isolated personality and increased his confidence while decreasing his anxiety. "All I have to do is wrap my hands around her, and everything is OK."

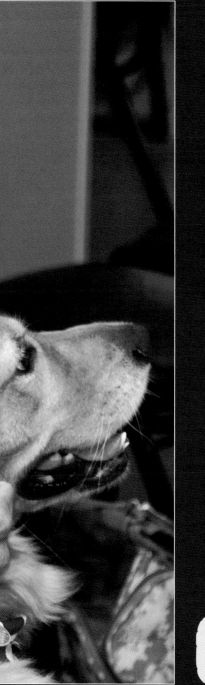

6

CANINE
CO-THERAPISTS

CANINE CO-THERAPISTS

Like her canine counterparts who deployed to Iraq and Afghanistan as COSC dogs, Lt. Col. Ilexy von Gruenberg helps veterans struggling with stress, anxiety, and the invisible wounds associated with PTSD. There are no plans to deploy Lexy, though, because this five-year-old German Shepherd Dog works her magic as Fort Bragg's first and only therapy dog. A conversation starter. An icebreaker. A medical tool. A canine co-therapist.

Partnered with owner-handler Maj. Christina Rumayor, the 82nd Airborne Division's psychiatrist, Lexy is trained to recognize elevations in an individual's anxiety. "If Lexy notices that a person is becoming more anxious or upset, she will naturally get up and go to that person so that the person can pet her, which is extremely calming for many people," says Rumayor.

The use of therapy dogs at military bases is relatively new. Plenty of research exists documenting the benefits of canine-assisted therapy. Simply petting a dog has been linked to reduced stress, anxiety, and blood pressure, and anecdotal examples of psychological benefits continue to be documented. While the cost of training a service dog is expensive, therapy dogs are usually trained by their owners with considerably less expense. Yet, not all commanders are on board with therapy dogs on base.

Recognizing that dogs can play a huge and important role in easing the counseling process for active-duty soldiers who are experiencing stress and anxiety is what prompted Rumayor to write the 2011 policy requesting to initiate the animal-assisted therapy program through Womack Army Medical Center at Fort Bragg. At that time, Lexy was already a certified therapy dog; in 2013, the policy passed, and Lexy went to work.

Lexy didn't start out as a therapy dog, and Rumayor didn't start out looking for one. While stationed in Hawaii, Rumayor looked at several puppies and noticed that eight-week-old Lexy had the curiosity and gentle temperament that she was looking for in a companion dog. The German Shepherd Dog breed's original function was to herd and work, yet millions of people fell in love with the movie exploits of Strongheart and Rin Tin Tin, and the breed became known for its loyalty, courage, loving disposition, and suitability as family pets.

Along the way, the German Shepherd Dog became the top choice for guide, police, and substance-detection work, roles it now shares with other equally capable breeds. Today, Lexy embodies the breed's legendary desire to please and is redefining the breed's role as a first-rate therapy dog.

Rumayor realized right away that Lexy had the traits conducive to therapy work: she was affectionate, attentive, calm, gentle, focused, quick to learn, and easy to train. When Lexy was around one year of age, Rumayor began shifting her training to focus more on therapy work, and, after about two years of schooling, Lexy became certified as Fort Bragg's first therapy dog. Today, she is a Lieutenant Colonel. (It's customary

As a certified therapy dog, Lexy instinctively knows when to lend a helping paw.

in the Army for dogs to outrank their handlers to prevent potential mishandling of the dogs, which would be tantamount to misconduct toward a senior-ranking soldier or officer.)

Despite Lexy's feminine yet intimidating good looks—chiseled head and long, strong muzzle—she naturally draws people in. She's always willing to accept a hug, a pet, or a kiss from soldiers needing comfort.

"Lexy's purpose in therapy sessions is very specific to what the patient needs," says Rumayor.

"Animal therapy can involve different counseling techniques for different people. When we combine it with traditional therapy, we find that it works and works well."

The human–canine bond is the core of animal-assisted therapy, and the efficacy of the dogs as healthcare tools greatly depends on how the dogs are trained and used by therapists and social workers. While a bit of mystery remains in the magic of the human–canine relationship, many warriors will tell you with absolute certainty that it is

While some may be intimidated by the German Shepherd Dog's powerful appearance, Lexy exudes friendliness and compassion.

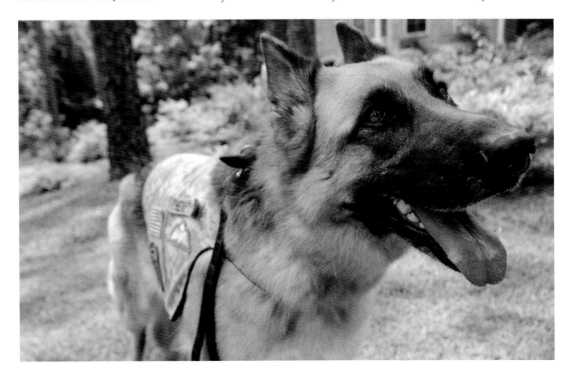

the unconditional, nonjudgmental love of a dog that gets them through the doors to Fort Bragg's Robinson Health Clinic. After all, who better to tell your problems to than a dog?

Not all soldiers talk, though. Some come just to see Lexy, to sit with her and pet her. Some talk not about deployments but about dogs, including their own dogs back home. Lexy gets them in front of a therapist, and that's a start. Once they show up for counseling, they are more likely to continue and comply with treatment, which is crucial for success.

Lexy's tail wags equally for everyone, privates and generals alike, and that alone can be a powerful tool, according to Rumayor. "Dogs have an unconditional type of love that brings [those seeking counsel] comfort. Dogs don't know what your rank is, and they don't care."

Lexy wears her therapy-dog vest with pride, eager to help the men and women who serve our country.

Lexy's therapy-dog Army combat vest sports plenty of badges, including the Parachutist Badge (commonly referred to as "jump wings"—a military badge of the United States Armed Forces) and the British Armed Forces Parachute Badge, as well as honorary Ranger and Special Forces tabs.

Sporting her vest, Lexy regularly accompanies Rumayor on walks around the base—to the motor pool or anywhere else soldiers might gather—to see if anyone is interested in talking. By interacting with troops not coming into the clinic, the soldiers may feel more comfortable becoming potential clients down the line. For Rumayor and Lexy, it's all about supporting the troops. On one occasion, Lexy made running a whole lot more fun when she showed up at 6:00 a.m. on a very cold morning to support more than 15,000 paratroopers who were running 4 miles to kick off All-American Week and boost morale.

Lexy is not the only military therapy dog. One hundred and forty five miles east and slightly south of Fort Bragg is United States Marine Corps Base Camp LeJeune, where licensed clinical social worker Donna Maglio is embedded with a battalion. Responsible for more than 900 Marines and sailors, Maglio notes that the battalion's previous therapist seldom, if ever, had service members make appointments or even take advantage of available drop-in schedules. His services simply were not utilized.

When Maglio took over, she needed to figure out how to get the active-duty men and women into her office. How best to gain their confidence and trust? How best to get them talking? How best to get them to set aside their bravado and seek treatment for a wide range of stress and mental-health issues brought on by more than a decade of war? After all, these men and women make up some of the finest fighting

Just stopping by to pet Lexy can often brighten someone's day.

forces in the world, and talking to a therapist is usually not high on their list of priorities.

Enter Neil: a nearly three-year-old Golden Retriever that Maglio acquired from Veterans Moving Forward in Alexandria, Virginia. Neil's career started as a potential service dog for an injured veteran. However, when he reached around one year of age, with roughly 75 percent of his training underway, Neil's minor hip issues deemed him ineligible for service-dog work. However, Neil's quintessential Golden Retriever temperament and gentle disposition proved a winning combination for therapy work. And, as it turns out, Neil is very good at calming active-duty service members who are struggling with stress and anxiety and getting them to open up—to talk.

Donna Maglio and Neil have made great strides in providing therapy for the Marines at Camp LeJeune.

Maglio continued with Neil's training. They completed his American Kennel Club (AKC) Canine Good Citizen requirements, and now Neil, who is named after Neil Armstrong, the first man to walk on the moon, is blazing his own trail as facility dog extraordinaire and the first unofficial battalion mascot.

"Neil interacts with a lot of people, and he has the ability to sense increased anxiety levels," says Maglio. "If a person is having an emotional conversation, Neil will get up, sit next to the person, rest his head on the person's lap, or lean on the person."

Before Neil, a few Marines came to see Maglio. Now a lot of them come to see Neil. "Neil instantly makes my day" and "This dog is awesome!" and "I just needed to come and hug Neil" and "It's a good Monday because of Neil" are just a sampling of the comments that Maglio hears on a regular basis. And then there are the customary greetings—"Hi, Neil!" and "What's up, Neil?"—that Maglio hears all day from people walking up and down the hallway while she's working at her desk. People also yell out to Neil from their cars in parking lots or while driving if they spot Maglio and Neil out for a walk. "On the days when I don't bring Neil to work, what I hear all day long is, 'Where's Neil?' and 'Will Neil be here tomorrow?'"

People want to spend time with Neil. He brings them joy, warmth, companionship, and smiles. And everyone who meets Neil has his or her favorite story. One Marine noted, "I almost failed uniform inspection this morning because I had a few dog hairs on my pants, but he let me pass because it was Neil's."

Attentive and affectionate, Neil immediately comforts those who seek Maglio's services.

So popular is Neil that people often bring him toys. Lots and lots of toys. At last count, he had eleven tennis balls, one lacrosse ball, one Kong, and one antler. One spouse made him a bandana, and some Marines made him a 550 paracord leash. Marines at Charlie Company want to install a doggie door for him, too.

The powerful influence dogs have on even the most hardened soldiers is illustrated in Napoleon Bonaparte's writings. His love–hate relationship with dogs is perhaps less recognized than his military exploits. In the early 1800s, when he was in exile and spending his time recording accounts of his days in battle, he wrote of one instance in which he was especially impressed by the strong bond between man and dog. In her book *General Howe's Dog*, author Caroline Tiger writes how Bonaparte was looking over a field littered with corpses. Next to one slain soldier sat a dog, licking his master's wounds. Profoundly moved, Bonaparte wrote:

Perhaps it was the spirit of the time and the place that affected me. But I assure you no occurrence of any of my other battlefields impressed me so keenly. I halted on my tour to gaze on the spectacle, and reflect on its meaning.

This soldier, I realized, must have had friends at home and in his regiment; yet he lay there deserted by all except his dog. . . . I had looked on, unmoved, at battles which decided the future of nations. Tearless, I had given orders which brought death to thousands.

Yet, here I was, stirred, profoundly stirred, stirred to tears. And by what? By the grief of one dog.

I am certain that at that instant I felt more ready than at any other time to show mercy toward a suppliant foeman. I could understand just then the tinge of mercy which led Achilles to yield the corpse of his enemy, Hector, to the weeping Priam.

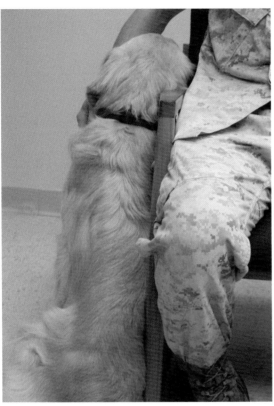

ABOVE: Neil offers a comforting presence just by being near a person who needs him.
ABOVE, RIGHT: Neil is as happy to see his Marine buddies as they are to see him.

The pattern of soldiers looking to dogs for support and dogs profoundly influencing soldiers is centuries old. While the use of facility/therapy dogs at military installations is relatively new, the practice is gaining acceptance. These hardworking dogs make it possible for therapists to connect with soldiers in ways that would have been extremely difficult, if not impossible, had the dogs not been present.

Dogs are making remarkable differences in the lives of modern-day soldiers on and off the battlefield. Consider, for example, that as a result of Lexy's success, Fort Bragg is hoping to expand its therapy-dog program in the behavioral-health clinics throughout the base. And, on a much larger scale, the Army is working to "support and standardize therapy-dog use throughout the military as it continues to gain momentum and prove beneficial in the lives of soldiers and veterans, as well as their families," according to "Maj. Rumayor and Lexy: Serving Our Country at Fort Bragg" an article in the Winter 2015 issue of *Pet Partners Interactions* magazine.

For as hard as Neil and Lexy work to help paratroopers, soldiers, Marines, and sailors cope, both Maglio and Rumayor recognize the importance of down time for the dogs.

"I never know if a session will be light or really emotional," says Maglio. "If Neil has had a particularly stressful day, he gets a full day off during the week, plus, of course, weekends, and lots of playtime. I can tell by looking at him when it's a good day to leave him at home."

Ditto for Lexy. "I never force Lexy to do her job," says Rumayor. "I'm very proactive, and if I notice her getting

Major Rumayor and Lexy serve an important purpose at Fort Bragg.

stressed, we take a break—go for a walk, tug, play ball, or down time in her crate, her own personal space."

Centuries-old memories prove that dogs have not only changed the course of history but have touched even the toughest of souls. Today's dogs—performing similar jobs but with modern-day training and titles—continue to touch and heal the wounded souls of our soldiers.

Major Rumayor recognizes the importance of giving Lexy some down time when she needs it.

JAMES KUIKEN
&
FREEDOM

It is a proud privilege to be a soldier—a good soldier…[with] discipline, self-respect, pride in his unit and his country, a high sense of duty and obligation to comrades and to his superiors, and a self confidence born of demonstrated ability.

~ George S. Patton Jr.

What are the odds that a stray dog facing euthanasia in a Kentucky shelter and a highly decorated combat-wounded veteran living in Virginia, struggling with the fallout from deployments into seven war zones, would find and save each other?

"I remember the moment I first met Freedom—my canine partner," says retired Sgt. Major James Kuiken. "I can't describe the overwhelming joy I felt when he came directly to me, licked my hand, and sat by my side. We quickly became inseparable and a completely bonded team."

The eighteen-month-old Labrador Retriever with the soft brown eyes melted the third-generation military man's heart with just one look.

James and Freedom became a team right from the start.

Joining the Marine Corps in 1973, Kuiken saw plenty of combat during his thirty years of military service, with deployments to Bosnia, Kosovo, Kuwait, Iraq, and Afghanistan. "My country was at war, and I wanted to do my part," says Kuiken.

In retrospect, Kuiken realized that he had PTSD and TBI issues in the late 1970s when he returned from his first deployment. Yet, like many active-duty and retired veterans, he didn't think that he needed help. He was strong enough to manage it on his own. After all, military service was in his blood. His father had spent thirty years in the US Air Force, and his grandfather was both Army and Navy. Kuiken himself is a highly decorated combat Marine, rising to the rank of Sergeant Major of Marine Forces Pacific, the highest Combatant Command in the Marines, overseeing two-thirds of the combat capabilities of the Marine Corps. His personal decorations include the Legion of Merit Medal, Purple Heart Medal, Navy and Marine Corps Commendation Medal, Navy and Marine Corps Achievement Medal, Army Achievement Medal, and Combat Action Ribbon with 2 Gold Stars as well as numerous campaign and service medals.

---

*Like many, Kuiken prefers the term PTS—post traumatic stress—choosing to eliminate the "disorder" label. While some experts consider PTS and PTSD two separate conditions, for consistency's sake throughout the book, the term PTSD is used and should not be viewed as judgmental or emblematic of a mental illness.

Freedom was rescued from a high-kill shelter and trained for PTSD service work by K9s For Warriors.

Looking back, Kuiken recognizes that he had been pulling away from his family and friends for years. However, after retiring from the military in 2003 and later from his job as the Department of Homeland Security Attaché to Iraq, his PTSD only got worse. He spent nearly all of his time sitting in a chair in his living room, sometimes for days at a time, doing nothing. "I didn't interact with other people or even my family," says Kuiken.

In 2014, in a "what-the-heck" kind of moment, Kuiken responded to a survey put out by Veterans 360, an organization that helps post-911 service members and veterans with PTSD and TBI.

"When my survey came back, the executive director called to ask if I was seeing anyone—concerned that I might be suicidal because I 'redlined' the survey. I've never been suicidal, but that got me thinking."

Kuiken realized that he was in a very dark place and needed help. Not only was he struggling with the invisible wounds of PTSD, he was also dealing with the physical fallout from multiple deployments into direct combat, including an explosion that had fractured his spine, damaged his heart and lungs, and blown out both of his knees. A TBI left him cognitively affected with vision, hearing, memory, and balance issues.

Knowing that Kuiken had had dogs all of his life, someone suggested that a companion dog might help Kuiken overcome his PTSD. Going online to research, he realized that he didn't need a companion dog—he needed a service dog.

Picked up by animal control as he roamed the streets with no identification—it's impossible to know with any certainty how Freedom, the young black Labrador Retriever, ended up in a high-kill shelter system with only a week or so to live. If he once had a home, he had been away from it for some time. His skin-and-bones physique suggested a scavenger's life. In a perfect world, someone might have rubbed his tummy, scratched his ears, and whispered sweet nothings in his ear. Yet, through no fault of his own, six-month-old Freedom had been blacklisted to a shelter, where he faced an insurmountable uphill battle.

Freedom was bailed out and sent to K9s For Warriors, a 501(c)(3) nonprofit organization in Ponte Vedra Beach, Florida, that rescues and trains primarily shelter dogs—both purebreds and mixed breeds. Founded in 2011 by Shari Duval, who was inspired by her son, a dog handler who returned from two tours in Iraq with PTSD, the organization has trained and donated more than 170 service dogs at no cost to active-duty troops and post-9/11 veterans suffering from PTSD or TBIs, helping them transition back to civilian life.

After completing six to eight months of basic obedience training and another four months of specialized training specific to wounded veterans, Freedom was ready to be matched with the right veteran. In the spring of 2014, Kuiken applied to K9s For Warriors, and in January 2015, after completing a detailed application and extensive vetting process, he traveled 750 miles south to Florida to spend three weeks immersed in the organization's intensive live-in program, during which he and Freedom would meet, bond, and train together. This included going on public outings to places such as movie theaters, restaurants, malls, and the like, which are all troublesome areas for most PTSD-affected veterans.

"I'm a 1-percenter," says Kuiken. "Most veterans have the same reaction triggers. They retreat, shut down, shy away. I'm part of the 1 percent that acts differently. I have no flight in the *fight-or-flight response*. I only have fight." (The fight-or-flight response is a healthy, automatic, inborn response that stimulates the adrenal glands, which in turn stimulate the release of adrenaline and noradrenaline, preparing both humans and animals to fight or flee from a perceived attack, harm, or threat to their survival.)

Kuiken's triggers are helicopters and loud, sharp noises, although, at one time, someone calling or coming to his front door could send him into a rage. Rather than

Having Freedom by his side helps Kuiken to stay calm.

"flee" from or try to avoid those triggers, Kuiken would instantly become aggressive in the direction of the trigger.

"Freedom's mellow personality counteracts my aggressive tendency," says Kuiken. "He reacts by stopping me. He'll lean into me or put his paw or butt on my foot. He pulls me out of it."

Many of the K9s For Warriors trainers are retired combat veterans. They are keenly aware of what PTSD-affected veterans are going through. They know the "choke points" and watch for them.

Like most veterans, Kuiken avoided crowds and noisy public venues. Anything moving above or behind him could trigger a full-blown panic attack, and that's what happened on his first training trip to the store with Freedom. Also accompanied by the organization's trainer, Kuiken had a major meltdown. Freedom picked up on subtle fluctuations in Kuiken's breathing and body language well ahead of the experienced trainer. "He put his paw in my lap and let me hug him," says Kuiken. "The staff took me outside and let me breathe a bit. Then we went back in."

In addition to mitigating the symptoms of PTSD, such as alerting Kuiken to people moving around behind him, Freedom's training also includes helping Kuiken with balance and mobility issues and retrieving medications. For instance, as a result of the TBI, standing with his feet too close together causes Kuiken to lose his balance and tip to the left, which is problematic because Kuiken doesn't realize when he's starting to fall. So in tune is Freedom to Kuiken's body language that he will put his foot or hind end on Kuiken's foot when he senses Kuiken's body start to shift or lean to the left.

During the three-week program at K9s For Warriors, Kuiken also had to learn how to work with Freedom, how to read him, and how to use him when he was feeling anxious. Upon returning home, they spent the first month working out any kinks and fine-tuning their working relationship. "At first, I thought [that Freedom] was being a pain in the butt," says Kuiken, "but then I realized what he was doing. He was distracting me. Every time he would see me react, he would do something to get my attention, to bring me back, to pull me out of it."

Freedom is a testament that good genetics and environment, coupled with proper training, can create a dog who does wonders when matched with the right person. Like in so many shelter-dog tales, the rescue dog became the rescuer, and Freedom and

Kuiken ended up saving each other. "Freedom was struggling with his own issues," says Kuiken. "He was fine at the training center, but once we were home, a few of his issues appeared. The first time I picked up a broom, he yipped and took off. When I playfully poked him with my toe, he started shaking and cowered. When I picked up a paper, he ran and hid in the corner."

Working together, they helped each other work through their separate issues. In doing so, they ended up saving each other. "He saved my life," says Kuiken. "He helped me to get out of a dark place."

Life changed dramatically for Kuiken in just the first six months since being matched with Freedom. Together twenty-four hours a day, seven days a week, Kuiken is more comfortable around people, especially in public. "Freedom opens me up emotionally," says Kuiken. "He makes me open up. I'm much more sociable. I actually talk to people now. I've reconnected with my family—my wife, kids, sisters, brother—people I hadn't communicated with in a long time."

While no scientific data exist regarding the relationship between rescued dogs and their owners, plenty of empirical and anecdotal data suggest that rescued dogs develop a deeper, more appreciative bond with their owners. "I've owned dogs all my life and nothing has approached the bond I have with Freedom. None of the other dogs came close to the deeply spiritual bond I have with Freedom."

A tireless advocate for wounded veterans, Kuiken writes (www.jameskuiken.com) and speaks publicly about the benefits of service dogs—what they can do, what they are doing to help our veterans and, in many instances, how they are saving our veterans lives.

"I am focused on saving these youngsters' lives," says Kuiken. "We have lost 6,600 soldiers in the Iraq and Afghanistan wars, which is tragic. Yet, we're losing twenty-two veterans a day to suicide. One veteran every 65 minutes. That's 8,000 veterans a year. We're losing more veterans to suicide each year than we did in ten years of war."

By sharing his story, Kuiken hopes that other veterans will seek help. " If I can step out and say, 'I need help,' then I am hoping others can, too."

Kuiken and Freedom share an unbreakable bond.

KATHY FELICE CHAMPION
&
GEORGE

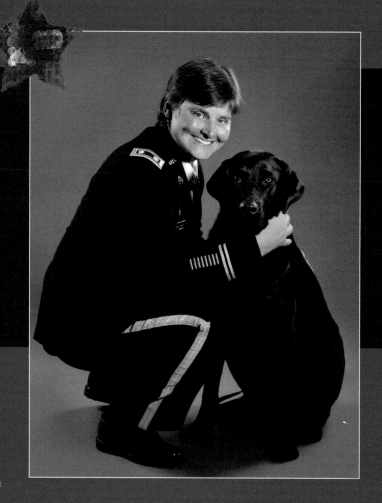

Our debt to the heroic men and valiant women in the service of our country can never be repaid. They have earned our undying gratitude. America will never forget their sacrifices.

~ President Harry S. Truman

Blind, deaf in one ear, and suffering from the long-term effects of multiple concussions, a broken back, torn shoulder and leg ligaments, and a severe case of PTSD, retired Lt. Col. Kathy Champion has only one regret. "I wish I were still in the military."

Medically retired after twenty-seven years of service, the "go get-'em kind of gal" who served in Afghanistan, Iraq, and four combat zones still struggles with civilian life. Awarded the Bronze Star for valor, the Meritorious Service Medal, the Army Commendation Medal, and a slew of additional ribbons and medals, Champion had her sights set on attaining the rank of general. All she wanted to do was be in the military. "I was crumbling. There were times I didn't know why I was alive," says Champion, who in 2013 attempted suicide.

Joining the US Army in 1982 as a reservist, Champion traveled a lot—Central America, Germany, Bosnia, Korea, Afghanistan, and Iraq. She commanded a civil affairs unit made up of thirty-two men. Called to active duty after the terror attacks of September 11, 2001, Champion and her fellow soldiers survived sniper attacks, ambushes, and explosions on a regular basis. On her first day in Iraq, she survived two IED explosions just traveling on Route Irish (once considered "the most dangerous highway in the world") to and from the Green Zone, a fortified area in central Baghdad where foreign embassies and government structures are located.

In May 2006, on the last ride of her last day in Iraq—which should have been an easy day—all hell broke loose. "We were going to hit the Green Zone and then return to Abu Ghraib," explains Champion. "This was the day I was handing over my area of operation to the new civil affairs unit." Champion recalls sniper fire from an AK-47 pinging off the medical building, raining down a terror of lead traveling at 2,300 feet per second—barely missing Champion and fellow soldiers as they entered it. Shortly thereafter, the same clinic was bombed.

Later that day, they were ambushed by insurgents leaving a council meeting. Yet her day was about to get much worse. About one mile outside of the safety of the Green

Angel and Kathy gave each other a new beginning.

Zone, an explosion from an IED brought mushroom clouds of dirt and smoke and chunks of metal spinning through the air.

Returning stateside, Champion struggled with the physical pain that accompanied her broken bones, fractured vertebrae, torn ligaments, and repeated concussions as well as the hidden psychological wounds: the flashbacks, nightmares, panic attacks, and social anxiety. A total of five men had died under her command during her military tour. "I feel like I failed those five people in combat," says Champion. "Maybe if I'd made different decisions, did things differently, they'd be home today rather than in a box."

Always athletic, Champion pushed herself physically and mentally to dull the pain by running marathons, including the 197-mile Hood to Coast (Oregon) relay race in 2007, yet her injuries were pulling her back. The marathon left her with agonizing pain from which she could not recover.

Excruciating lower back pain, muscle weakness, and paralysis are hallmark symptoms of transverse myelitis, a neurological disorder caused by inflammation across both sides of one level, or segment, of the spinal cord. Often the result of a virus, transverse myelitis can lead to sensory deprivation. The virus attacked Champion's optic nerve, destroying her vision. Traced back to Iraq, the virus was most likely a result of the endless sandstorms. However, Champion says that walking through all sorts of disgusting conditions, including sewage, wasn't unusual, and that she could have contracted it anywhere in Iraq.

A decorated military veteran, world traveler, paramedic/emergency medical technician, and college graduate who holds two master's degrees, Champion felt defined by her injuries and loss of vision. "Who wants to hang out with a blind person?" Once fiercely independent, athletic, and proud, Champion plummeted into depression, rarely leaving her Gulfport, Florida, home. "I lost faith in humanity. I lost faith in myself. I lost the happy-go-lucky gal I once was."

Transverse Myelitis

Transverse myelitis often develops following viral infections, according to the National Institute of Neurological Disorders and Stroke's Transverse Myelitis Fact Sheet. Infectious agents suspected of causing transverse myelitis include varicella zoster (the virus that causes chicken pox and shingles), herpes simplex, cytomegalovirus, Epstein-Barr, influenza, echovirus, human immunodeficiency virus (HIV), hepatitis A, and rubella. Bacterial skin infections, middle-ear infections (otitis media), and Mycoplasma pneumoniae (bacterial pneumonia) have also been associated with the condition.

Kathy and George's bond began at the beach.

Like a deflating balloon, Champion's life energy was slipping away. Her strained relationship with her daughter, who had been sixteen years old when Champion deployed and was eighteen when she returned, became further estranged. "It was a bad period in my life. I was all alone."

In 2008, five friends stopped by, coaxing her out of the house under false pretenses. Planning to stop by Southeastern Guide Dogs, the friends kept that a secret from Champion. That day marked the beginning of a new journey—and a new Champion.

Her saving grace, or guardian angel, so to speak, was a guide dog named Angel.

Champion's search for a guide dog had plenty of quirky twists and turns that seemed to be more than just coincidence. For starters, bred and trained specifically for guide-dog work, Angel had already been unsuccessfully matched with two previous handlers. "I was Angel's third and last shot," says Champion. "If she didn't make it with me, she was going back to the puppy raiser." Also, Champion's nickname for her daughter is "Angel."

Living at Southeastern Guide Dogs' Palmetto, Florida, campus for twenty-six days taught Champion how to work with Angel, how to become a team, and how to navigate real-world situations, such as going to the grocery store, airport, train station, and elsewhere. Putting her sight-impaired life in the hands of a dog required Champion to have an enormous amount of trust. As Champion took her first steps, she relinquished all control entirely to Angel. "I was more terrified of walking with Angel than stepping on an explosive in Iraq," says Champion. "After those first few steps, I knew she would not put me into the ditch."

Returning to her Gulfport home, Champion's life took on a rarefied air of normalcy, doing for herself instead of asking others. She and Angel were a perfect match. "We were alone. It was just me and Angel. Sharing my frustrations, she listened to me."

Angel became Champion's eyes and emotional soul. Her confidante. Her therapist. She restored Champion's spirit, renewed her self-confidence, and provided her with the independence and freedom she thought she'd forever lost. With Angel by her side, Champion began traveling again—ice climbing, hiking in the Grand Canyon, and sailing. Angel became the first dog to attend Space Camp in Huntsville, Alabama, experiencing zero gravity and flying in F-16 and F-18 fighter-jet simulators.

Still struggling with physical and emotional injuries, including a fear of crowds, Champion pushed herself by becoming a public speaker and a relentless advocate for disabled veterans. During a 2011 workshop in Montana at which Champion was speaking about the benefits of service dogs and how they can help injured veterans find their inner selves again, Champion and Angel (in harness) took a short walk across a courtyard. To the shock of all watching, another dog attacked Angel. Champion began to panic and experience flashbacks. People rushed to her aid.

Angel suffered a bite to her hindquarters. Adding insult to injury, the owner of the other dog blamed Angel. The incident left Angel traumatized, and she would growl anytime she saw another dog. "We could never shake her of that," says Champion.

Angel was forced into early retirement. Knowing that she would need another guide dog and physically unable to care for two dogs at the same time, Champion reluctantly sent Angel to live with the woman who had devoted so much time to raising and socializing her as a puppy.

Champion's "heart dog" was gone. Spiraling into a serious depression, she isolated herself, drank too much, and, in January 2013, facing a seemingly irreversible spin, she attempted suicide. "Afterward, I thought, 'What's wrong with me?' Suicide is just stupid!"

Needing a new dog, Champion eventually returned to Southeastern Guide Dogs. She wasn't happy. She looked at twenty-eight guide dogs, and none of them, in Champion's opinion, was right for her. None of them were Angel. Someone even admonished her: "Your next dog is not going to be Angel! Get over it."

The twenty-ninth dog was George, an energetic eighteen-month-old black Labrador Retriever. "I think this is the dog for me," declared Champion. Returning to Gulfport, she completed a two-week home-placement program (because she had previously owned a service dog, she did not have to complete the twenty-six-week on-campus training). She and George spent their first weekend playing, walking on the beach, and bonding. "I drank only one beer at night instead of getting drunk!"

Champion felt connected again. Falling in love with George, she was ready to start a new journey with him. George has been at her side ever since. "George took me back to where I should have been. Where I let myself fall away from." (In another interesting twist, George was born on Veterans Day, 11/11/11. Champion's son was also born on Veterans Day. And Champion's ex-husband's name is George!)

George helped Kathy regain her confidence and pursue what she loves to do.

Like many veterans, Champion has issues with crowds. When people get too close and memories of the past come crashing in, George always has her back. His presence and his touch keep Champion rooted in the present.

George serves a dual purpose, and he's always on his game with an enthusiastic sense of duty. A strong human–canine bond has resulted in George's performing behaviors for which he was never trained, including emotional support and nightmare interruption. For example, George will paw Champion's chest or lay his head across her neck to wake her up, and these are responses for which George had no specialized training.

At fifty years old and still struggling with her injuries, Champion recognizes that she can't change the past nor can she live in the past. A shining beacon to those wrestling with emotional and physical disabilities, Champion sets high standards for herself. Most sighted people—even those half her age—would have trouble keeping up with her lifestyle. In addition to volunteering as a public speaker to raise awareness about guide and service dogs for disabled veterans, she remains an avid athlete, hiking and sailing. Her team took first place in the 2014 US Disabled Sailing Triplehanded Championship, Sonars/A-Fleet division. She also bikes, swims, and runs, finishing first in the 2014 St. Anthony's Triathalon's "female physically challenged" division, in which she rode a tandem bicycle with an able-bodied cyclist and swam and ran while tethered to an able-bodied partner.

Although George is not with Champion while she competes, he is always by her side otherwise, helping her before and after competitions. Currently, she is training with the goal of competing in the 2016 Paralympic Games in Rio de Janeiro, in which the paratriathlon will makes its debut. "People think I can't do something because I'm blind," says Champion. "What do they know about it?"

These days, Champion is all about encouraging other veterans to get outside and get active. "I can show people, 'Look, she's not 100 percent, and she's certainly not twenty years old anymore, but she's participating with a bunch of people and being active,'" says Champion. "I went from commanding men and women in combat to being told that I would never walk again. My new purpose is to encourage people to step out of their dark holes and become alive again."

Environment of War

A study published by the American Psychological Association that focused on non-combat-related ailments provided information about the environmental conditions to which deployed service members are exposed. These conditions include poor food quality, poor air quality (burning trash and feces, smoke from oil-well fires, and so forth), and flies and insect-borne diseases including leishmaniasis, a parasitic cutaneous infection caused by a sand fly endemic to both Afghanistan and Iraq.

Is there any doubt that this pair was meant to be together?

Champion adds, "They told me, 'This is your new normal. Get used to it.' I hate that phrase 'new normal.' No! This is what my life is, and I have accepted that, and now I'm going to use whatever opportunities to be in the moment and try something I've never tried before."

Champion's passion and enthusiasm for life are infectious. So, too, are her smile, laughter, and quirky sense of humor. As a frequent traveler, she usually has an escort take her to the hotel, show her the room, and take her back to the lobby, where the hotel staff members always ask, "Do you need any help?" To which Champion replies, "No. My dog has everything under control."

Champion admits that she still misses the Army. She's proud of her military service and equally proud of what she has accomplished in her civilian life. "What I do now means a lot. It matters. I'm helping other vets, and that's important." She's quick to add that most people will never know what George means to her and how his life-changing companionship helps her to appreciate each day by giving her confidence, independence, and freedom. "I will always have a dog. Dogs are my salvation. George makes me see the present, so I don't live in the past."

7

FROM SHELTER TO SERVICE

FROM SHELTER TO SERVICE

The stories are poignant and seemingly endless.
A rescued dog helps an Iraqi war veteran suffering from
PTSD manage his anxiety in stressful situations. A once-
homeless shelter dog coping with his own stress finds
a new life as a much-loved companion helping a PTSD-
affected Army officer. An Air Force officer suffering with a
deep and prolonged depression regains a sense of purpose
in his life thanks to an adopted shelter dog. A Vietnam
veteran and Purple Heart recipient diagnosed with cancer
and muscular dystrophy finds stability with a once-abused
and abandoned dog.

The practice of training shelter dogs as service dogs is
becoming more commonplace, but despite the estimated
3.9 million dogs entering shelters each year, finding the
right dog for the right task and matching that dog to a
veteran is more challenging than one might expect.

The high cost of breeding purebred dogs who are physically
and temperamentally sound, the enormous time commitment
and the number of volunteers needed for puppy raising and
socialization, and the long waiting times, which can be up
to two years, have some service-dog organizations turning
to junior and adult dogs in shelters as a ready source of

inexpensive, trainable canines for people who need service dogs.

One such program is Shelter to Solider, a 501 (c)(3) nonprofit in San Diego, California, that rescues shelter dogs and trains them to become certified service dogs for wounded veterans. The dogs are trained to alleviate stress, anxiety, sleeplessness, hypervigilance, panic attacks, and other symptoms related to PTSD and TBIs.

The cost to train a shelter dog to mitigate the effects of PTSD or TBI averages $8,000 to $10,000, depending on the behaviors that the dog is specifically trained to perform, such as blocking, backing, hugging, interrupting nightmares, responding to seizures, pulling a wheelchair, hitting a 911 button, opening doors, and retrieving personal items (e.g., car keys, eyeglasses, cell phones, and so forth). Compare that to guide dogs, which are almost always selectively bred and trained for their work at a cost of $50,000 to $70,000.

For some organizations, such as K9s For Warriors, a 501 (c)(3) nonprofit in Ponte Vedra Beach, Florida, the cost averages $15,000 to $20,000 per dog-and-veteran team, which includes a comprehensive three-week live-in training program. During this time, previously screened veterans and dogs meet, bond, and learn, together with their trainers, in order to practice and hone their newfound skills. This training includes working on alleviating or escaping stressful situations out in public, such as in movie theaters, restaurants, malls, and the like.

Other contributing factors that can increase or decrease the cost of training include the amount of basic obedience training a dog had before he ended up in the shelter. In the case of Miley (see page 192), the Golden Retriever mix who had already been through advanced training before she was

A mixed-breed dog with the proper temperament can be a superstar service dog.

owner-surrendered to the Virginia shelter, the time and cost involved was significantly reduced.

Whether dogs come from shelters or breeding programs, the majority of money to support the organizations that train them for service work comes from individual donors, businesses, foundations, community groups, fundraising, and so forth. Most, but certainly not all, reputable organizations provide the dogs to veterans at no cost.

Potential service dogs need to have confident, stable, and friendly temperaments.

"There are millions of reasons for this [type of] program," says animal behavior expert Sherry Woodard, who runs Utah's Best Friends Animal Society's Canines with Careers program, which trains shelter and rescue dogs in jobs that benefit people, thus saving the dogs' lives as well. In 2013, Best Friends placed more than 380 canines in jobs helping people. "Every day, thousands of dogs are dying in shelters across the country, simply because they are homeless. At the same time, millions of people with psychiatric disabilities don't have the service dogs they need."

An article in the March/April 2015 issue of *Best Friends Magazine* profiles US Army veteran Paul Lloyd, who had been looking for more than a year for the right dog to train as his service animal. After several visits to Best Friends Pet Adoption Center in Salt Lake City, Lloyd met Rex, a cute red dog with a calm demeanor who accepted Lloyd on the spot. Lloyd changed Rex's name to Cowboy, and the rescued dog quickly settled into his new home. The first night, he refused to leave Lloyd's side. Cowboy has started his training to become a certified PTSD dog, and Lloyd says that Cowboy is a fast learner and is already proving to be a loving, caring, and patient friend.

Dogs end up in shelters for all sorts of reasons, through little or no fault of their own. Some dogs become separated and lost from their owners. Sometimes an owner dies and has no relatives who are willing or able to take the dog. Some dogs escape through open gates or holes in fences. Some dogs are abandoned, and others are picked up or seized by animal control.

Dogs learn a foundation of basic obedience before moving on to specialized service training.

Shelter dogs are not broken or bad, nor are they stupid or imperfect, according to trainer and behavioral expert Robert Cabral, author of the book *Desperate Dogs, Determined Measures: Helping Shelters Save More Lives* (2012). "Dogs end up in shelters because the expectation that [the humans] put upon them was just too much, and, most importantly—people have not properly bonded with their dogs."

A study by Mo D. Salman et al. titled "Behavioral Reasons for Relinquishment of Dogs and Cats to Twelve Shelters," published in 2000 in the *Journal of Applied Animal Welfare Science*, indicates that the top behavioral reasons dogs are surrendered to animal shelters include:

- acting aggressively toward people and/or other animals
- chasing animals and/or cars
- being too active
- needing too much attention
- vocalizing too much
- escaping
- disobeying
- displaying destructive behavior inside or outside the house
- jumping on people

The same study notes that 39–50 percent of the dogs relinquished to shelters for behavioral reasons were originally acquired from shelters. Other data indicate that an estimated 25 percent of dogs in shelters are purebreds, and the majority of dogs surrendered to shelters are between one and two years of age, which corresponds with the "teenage" phase of many breeds.

Trainers say it can take a lot of time—sometimes a year or more—and a lot of energy to decode a dog's temperament and sometimes quirky behaviors—in other words, why he does what he does. Why he's submissive, fearful, reactive, or skittish. Why he cowers at the sight of men in floppy hats, people in wheelchairs, or small children flailing their arms.

Most unbelievably, the study also uncovered these alarming statistics:

- 88.1 percent of owners relinquishing dogs to shelters indicated that they never took their dogs to obedience classes
- 75.7 percent of the owners say that their dogs did not know basic obedience commands when they adopted them
- 91.8 percent of the owners say that they did not have professional trainers train their dogs
- 91.3 percent of owners (including family members) never received individual obedience instructions
- 69.7 percent of the dogs had not been taught basic commands

K9s For Warriors is not deterred by statistics. Founded in
2011 by Shari Duval, who was inspired by her son, a dog
handler who returned home with PTSD after two tours in
Iraq, the organization has trained and donated more than 170
service dogs at no cost to active-duty troops and post-9/11
veterans suffering from PTSD or TBIs.

Ninety-five percent of K9s For Warriors' dogs are rescued
from shelters—many within weeks or even days of being
euthanized. Twenty-two veterans a day—that's one veteran
every sixty-five minutes—commits suicide, with 31 percent
of these suicides being veterans forty-nine years old or
younger. Thus, K9s For Warriors' goal is to save the lives of
both dogs and veterans. Such was the case with Freedom,
a gentle, affectionate black Labrador Retriever rescued from
a high-kill animal shelter in Kentucky a week or so before
he was scheduled to be euthanized. Now a certified PTSD

service dog, Freedom is paired with a multiple-war Marine Corps veteran who served in seven war zones and has struggled with PTSD. A dog saved. A vet saved.

Data on the number of shelter dogs adopted and trained for service work are scarce. However, Paws With A Cause, a 501 (c) (3) nonprofit organization in Wayland, Michigan, that custom-trains service dogs as well as hearing dogs and seizure-response dogs, found the following by analyzing their own data: "Our organization has very stringent standards," says Portasue Hendrickson, Director of Administration. "Our success rate with shelter dogs is only one in twelve or fifteen dogs. Other organizations may have different data depending on their criteria."

Although Paws With A Cause continues to work closely with local animal shelters to rescue adult dogs—between fourteen months and three years old—the low rate of success is why the organization established its own limited strategic breeding program. By contrast, roughly 90 percent of the 100 or so puppies whelped each year by the organization go on to succeed as either service or working dogs. Dogs who are not utilized by the organization are offered to Leader Dogs for the Blind, a nonprofit that trains dogs for the visually impaired, as well as to the Department of Homeland Security, military agencies, and police agencies.

Freedom was rescued from a high-kill shelter and trained for PTSD service work by K9s For Warriors.

Although Paws With A Cause includes shelter dogs in its programs, the organization typically works with purebreds, such as Labrador Retrievers (pictured), for service-dog training. New students Emmett (BELOW) and Tonka (BELOW, RIGHT) are ready to learn.

"Why breed dogs when there are so many homeless dogs in shelters?" It's a question that trainers hear frequently, and while their hearts go out to the dogs in shelters, the number-one priority of most organizations that train service dogs is to help people with disabilities by providing them with well-trained dogs with sound temperaments. More often than not, many smaller organizations simply do not have the time or manpower to screen hundreds of shelter dogs and pick out the relatively few gems who will succeed as service dogs.

Because K9s For Warriors trains dogs for veterans with PTSD and TBIs, they are looking for specific height, weight, size, and temperament traits. This type of specificity allows the organization to work with a number of shelters, in and out of state, that know exactly what type of dogs they require. Ninety percent of dogs that K9s For Warriors trains are mixed breeds, with the organization accepting almost any breed or mixed breed as long as the dog weighs 60 pounds, stands 24 inches tall, is at least one year of age, and meets the necessary temperament/personality requirements.

Many of the organizations, including Paws With A Cause, primarily use selectively bred dogs, such as Golden Retrievers and Labrador Retrievers, but are not opposed to using the right shelter dogs. "We look for smaller purebreds or mixed breeds at shelters for our hearing-dog program," says Hendrickson. Small dogs are often favored for hearing-dog work because they can jump into a person's lap to alert them to sounds, whereas the size and strength of larger dogs are better suited to service work, which includes helping their owners balance, pulling wheelchairs, tugging open doors, and other physical tasks.

The need for trained service dogs is growing—especially among veterans, with a 2008 RAND Corporation study reporting that one in five soldiers returning from Afghanistan and Iraq is suffering from PTSD. A summary by the Pew Research Center puts the number at nearly four in ten soldiers (37 percent) reporting that they believe they have

Because service work can be physically demanding, training organizations usually choose larger dogs.

suffered from PTSD. TBIs are the signature injury of the two wars, with data indicating that 19.5 percent of 300,000 returning military service members reported experiencing a TBI while deployed, and 7 percent reported both a probable brain injury and current PTSD or major depression. Other data indicate that individuals with a TBI are one and a half times more likely than healthy individuals to die from suicide, according to Dr. Margaret C. Harrell and Nancy Berglass in "Losing the Battle: The Challenge of Military Suicide" on the Center for a New American Security's website (www.cnmas.org) in October 2011.

For a veteran needing a service dog, the wait can be as long as two years. In addition to cost and availability, organizations must match the right dog with the right task and owner. The process is not an exact science, and mismatches are potentially costly and time-consuming. PTSD manifests in different ways, and some trainers voice concern about pairing a shelter dog who has an unknown history and unproven temperament with a veteran struggling with his own emotional issues. Citing a lack of proven data, they say there is a lot potential for things to go wrong. However, when chosen correctly, shelter dogs are proving to be worthy service dogs. To improve the odds of choosing correctly, trainers employ a series of temperament tests.

During World War II, the Guide Dogs for the Blind school became the first to develop a selection tool for service dogs. In the 1940s, C. J. Pfaffenberger and John Paul Scott, also from Guide Dogs for the Blind, developed a puppy test based on the social genetics of the dogs and how the behavioral development of dogs could be divided into different stages— the neonatal, transitional, socialization, juvenile, pubertal, and parental—based on social changes in the puppy.

This test proved successful in improving the success rate of dogs entering and completing guide-dog training. (Many suggest that failure rates can be misleading because most dogs who do not meet the criteria for guide-dog work become "career change" dogs and go into other types of service-dog work or substance-detection work or breeding programs.)

Plenty of similar tests have come along since Pfaffenberger and Scott, with proponents and opponents on both sides of the efficacy issue. One drawback to these tests is that they were developed for puppies, not for adult shelter dogs. Plus, shelters are notoriously stressful for dogs, and assessing a dog's true temperament and personality in a shelter environment can be challenging, especially when the dogs first arrive.

By observing a dog's body language, a trainer can tell a lot about what the dog might be thinking. Is he relaxed, withdrawn, assertive, fearful? Are his eyes darting around the room? How does he relate to his environment and the people and other animals around him? Will he take a treat? How does he respond to noise, such as clicking sounds, doors

closing, or a clipboard falling on the ground? Does he engage or frighten quickly and easily?

Trainers often use a combination of tasks to assess a dog's behavior, including his behavior in the kennel, how he walks on leash, and how he reacts to novel stimuli, such as an umbrella opening, a stranger passing by, hands clapping, and the like.

"We look for different things depending on the task the dog will perform," explains Hendrickson. "We want a dog who is not easily frightened. A dog who is submissive, but not overly submissive to the point of submissively pottying on the floor. We look for dogs who are not territorial or reactive and do not have protection or aggressive issues or resource guarding tendencies. The dogs must be eager to please, have a natural tendency to look to humans for instructions, and be command driven."

Trainers generally look for dogs between fourteen months and three years old. Very few organizations select puppies of unknown history because it can take twelve to eighteen months

A good service-dog candidate must stay focused on the task at hand.

to know how a puppy will turn out. Although Labrador Retrievers and Golden Retrievers, either purebred or mixed-breed, are the dogs of choice, it's rare to find them in shelters.

Like their selectively bred canine counterparts, shelter dogs must undergo and pass veterinary health checks, be free of heartworm disease and allergies, and have good hips and elbows. Several orthopedic conditions can cause structural instability, with hip dysplasia and elbow dysplasia being top concerns. These conditions are frequently seen in medium and large breeds and can cause weakness and lameness resulting in arthritis, debilitating pain, and crippling. The time and expense involved in training service dogs excludes all but the emotionally and physically fit dogs. However, dogs with minor hip or elbow issues are not necessarily excluded from all canine work. Some work in less physically demanding roles, such as therapy or comfort dogs.

According to a 2013 report by the Committee on the Assessment of the Readjustment Needs of Military Personnel, Veterans, and Their Families, as of December 2010, Operation Enduring Freedom (OEF) in Afghanistan and Operation Iraqi Freedom (OIF) in Iraq resulted in the deployment of about 2.2 million troops. As soldiers continue to return home, there remains no shortage of wounded warriors or shelter dogs who need our help. Specially trained shelter dogs are one way to reduce the number of veterans dying each day by suicide while simultaneously helping injured veterans return to civilian life with dignity and independence—and the dogs' lives are saved, too.

IRWIN STOVROFF
&
CASH

"Freedom is not free. For all of us who are enjoying the freedom that we have in this country today, somebody paid the price, and it becomes your obligation to help them for their future and their lives."

~Irwin Stovroff, WWII Veteran

August 13, 1944: The thirty-fifth mission was a "milk run"—a trip over the English Channel to the town of Falaise, France, which is famous for the battle that encircled the German army, creating a pocket known as the *Falaise Pocket*, from which, for the Germans, there would be no escape. "We were going to blow up these bridges blocking the Germans from escaping the coastline in Normandy. I was lining up my bomb site and—wham!—we got hit," says Irwin Stovroff, a then twenty-two-year-old second lieutenant and bombardier in the US Air Force.

German 88-mm shells from anti-aircraft guns tore through the American B-24 Liberator's number-one and -two engines, creating a trail of black smoke and flames and disabling the plane's hydraulic system. Stovroff toggled the 1,000-pound bombs through the bomb-bay doors, stripped off his flak jacket, strapped on a parachute, and, along with the nine crew members, bailed out of the battle-damaged heavy bomber. Counting—*eight, nine, ten*—he pulled the parachute's ripcord. Dropping 18,000 feet, he

hit the ground and tossed his dog tags that were stamped with "H" for Hebrew. Landing on Nazi-occupied soil, Stovroff had German guns trained on him almost immediately.

Together, the *Passion Pit*'s crew flew thirty-four bombing missions—many deep into Germany, bombing every major target in Germany, including raids on Berlin. Originally, they were told that they would fly twenty-five missions during the war, but due to the high casualty rate, that number climbed to thirty and then thirty-five. The thirty-fifth mission was the crew's last scheduled assignment before completing their tour of duty. Instead of returning stateside, however, Stovroff ended up at Stalag Luft 1, spending thirteen months as a POW.

In a twist stranger than fiction, Stovroff recounts how one of the Nazi interrogators had grown up around the corner from his home in Buffalo, New York. "Your father's name is Max, your mother's name is Bertha. You have a brother, Morton, and a sister named Irma," the interrogator told him. Speaking perfect English, he then rattled off the name of the high school from which Stovroff had graduated and even the name of the girl he had dated before joining the Air Force. He had gone to school with Stovroff's older sister, and it turned out that Stovroff had once been the paperboy for the Nazi interrogator's parents. He explained to Stovroff how he had returned to Germany with his grandmother and had stayed.

On the pink paperwork, the interrogator put a question mark next to Stovroff's Jewish religion. That act may have saved Stovroff's life.

Despite the horrific conditions, Stovroff remained optimistic until February 1945, when Adolf Hitler began segregating Jewish Air Force officers. Anyone who was remotely close to being Jewish would be killed. Before Stovroff could be executed, the POW camp was liberated by Russian Cossacks, and eventually he returned home to the United States.

"What we were trying to do was save the world, and we did," he told *Fox News*' Sean Hannity during an interview. "I was young and wanted to do my part."

Returning stateside, Stovroff graduated from the University of Illinois in 1948, married, raised a family, and went on to a busy business career until retiring in 1997 at seventy-five years old.

Seventy-one years after parachuting out of the B-24 Liberator over Nazi-occupied France, the ninety-three-year-old Stovroff—recipient of the Air Medal, the Purple Heart, and the Distinguished Flying Cross, which was presented by ex-prisoner of war Senator John McCain—is still at work, still grateful to be alive, and still serving our nation by helping returning veterans adjust to civilian life after war.

In the Air Force, Stovroff became part of the Mighty 8th Air Force—the greatest air armada in history—eventually being assigned to the 44th Bomb Group, where he and nine crew members flew the four-engine plane designed for high-altitude bombing. This photo of Stovroff's B-24 going down on August 13, 1944, was taken by a friend and sent to Stovroff's parents.

Like most veterans, Stovroff balks at the term "hero." "I'm very proud of the fact that I really did do something in combat for my country. I recognize that I am a very fortunate man," says Stovroff. "I came home in one piece. Being Jewish, I was lucky to get out of there alive. I've never forgotten that. So I spend my time helping those who can't help themselves."

Stovroff decided that there was more to retirement than his tennis game. Volunteering at the West Palm Beach (Florida) Veterans Administration Center as a National Service Officer, he, along with a friend, helped more than 400 ex-POWs with pensions and medical claims. In 2006, at eighty-four years old, he began volunteering with the blind rehabilitation program at the Veterans Hospital in Palm Beach, where he learned that the government provides no funding for the training of service dogs for veterans struggling with physical or emotional injuries, including TBI and PTSD—two of the most significant injuries sustained by veterans returning from Iraq and Afghanistan. "I couldn't believe it!"

Stovroff has had dogs his entire life, so when he was asked to find organizations that raise and train dogs for the blind and disabled, and what it would cost, he knew that it was the job for him. What he found was that it costs a lot of money to raise and train service dogs. So he went to every single veterans' organization he knew, and they all came together to raise $100,000 in three months.

Determined to make sure that every veteran who needs a dog will be able to get one of his or her own, Stovroff founded Vets Helping Heroes, a 501(c)(3) nonprofit foundation that raises funds that are then donated to nonprofit organizations that train service dogs for veterans.

Stovroff has experienced firsthand the difference that a service dog can make in a veteran's life. Prior to Stovroff's founding Vets Helping Heroes, Cash, a purebred

LEFT TO RIGHT: Irwin Stovroff (with service dog Cash and therapy dog Jenny), Bob Engelman, Sam Bierstock, Don Werner, Lou Moline, Paul Berreto, Charlie Morgenstein, and Mel Pollack (not pictured: John Van Blois and Kathy Genovese).

The bond between Irwin and Cash is so strong that they understand each other's verbal communication and body-language signals.

Golden Retriever, was placed with Stovroff though America's VetDogs (AVD), a 501(c)(3) organization that trains service dogs for injured veterans as well as civilians. A heart murmur excluded Cash from the AVD guide-dog program, yet his quintessential Golden-Retriever temperament, devotion, and willingness to work made him the ideal service-dog ambassador—the "poster canine" for others in need. Never far from Stovroff's side, Cash also helps to mitigate the effects of PTSD, which Stovroff continues to live with from his time as a POW.

"A trained PTSD dog will get right up in your face when he smells your mood change," explains Stovroff in Lisa A. Weiser's book, *An Extraordinary Life…Gone to the Dogs.* "He will buffer you from the stress of crowds and place himself between you and the stranger. When you come home to the shadows that lurk within your home, he would advance into a room and turn on the lights. The security to know you are safe is invaluable, and the constant supervision from a friend that protects you from yourself is even greater. There is no loyalty like [that] from a dog. They have your back and your heart and give people another way to cope with their despair."

According to Stovroff, half of the deaths at Normandy were due to bleeding, and 20 percent of those could have been prevented with the right equipment and training.

Advances in body armor, weaponry, strategy, technology, transportation, and battlefield medicine have given troops a better chance of coming home alive. For the first time in American history, large percentages of injured soldiers returning from the battlefield are surviving their injuries.

Since 2007, Vets Helping Heroes has raised $4.5 million and funded the training of 120 dogs for our nation's wounded veterans.

BACK: Mel Pollack (left), Vets Helping Heroes board member and former POW of the Vietnam War; and Don Werner (right), Vets Helping Heroes board chair. FRONT: Lt. Col. Kathy Champion and George (left) and Irwin Stovroff and Cash (right).

While the dogs are provided at no cost to veterans, the cost of raising and training a dog ranges between $10,000 and $60,000 per dog—depending on the level of training required. The average cost of a guide dog, for example, runs about $60,000 (although some experts put the figure as high as $70,000), whereas training for a therapy/facility dog averages about $10,000. Currently, Vets Helping Heroes provides funding to five nonprofit organizations that breed, raise, and train dogs for our nation's veterans who are disabled, be it loss of vision or hearing, loss of limb(s), seizures, PTSD, or TBI.

Stovroff shares how one day he was called to the hospital. A young veteran—thirty-two years old—had been blinded in combat. "I don't want to go home," he told Stovroff. "I'm a handicap to my wife and kids." Beside Stovroff was Cash, his ever-present service dog. "I told him that if he had his own dog, he'd have mobility, companionship, and independence, and that his kids were going to have a great pet." The veteran recovered and now has a new life. "It's a remarkable story, and I'm so happy to be a part of it."

Stovroff believes in the powerful love that is found just by looking into a dog's eyes.

On a separate occasion, Stovroff recounts how a veteran struggling with seizures was teetering on the brink of suicide. The man's wife was completely convinced that he would kill himself. "He received a dog, and his life has completely changed," says Stovroff. "It's wonderful to see the beginning of a life together when a veteran receives a service dog."

Additionally, the organization has funded the training of four facility dogs, including Bruce, a two-year-old black Labrador Retriever. Trained by Sam Argo, who works at Southeastern Guide Dogs in Palmetto, Florida, Bruce's quintessential breed characteristics—stable temperament and willingness to please—proved a winning combination for therapy-dog work. Monday through Friday, Bruce visits about 100 military veterans who live at the West Palm Beach VA Hospital's Community Living Center. He provides companionship, which, in turn helps ward off depression and loneliness and, in some instances, the anxiety and stress that accompany PTSD. Plenty of research exists to document the benefits of therapy dogs, including reduced stress, anxiety, and blood pressure, and anecdotal examples of psychological benefits continue to be documented. "Three months after Bruce was at the hospital," says

Stovroff, "the doctor called and told me, 'You know, Irwin, all of my patients' blood pressure has gone down.'"

Each day, Bruce and his handler, Chaplain Gary Leopard, clock out at about 4 pm. Leopard takes Bruce home each night, and weekends are his days off—time to just be a dog, hang out, and play.

Stovroff shows no signs of slowing down. Every day, he is promoting the benefits of service dogs for wounded veterans. He explains that if a disabled veteran is giving up in life, if he or she is suicidal, and Vets Helping Heroes can prove to that veteran that a dog can do what modern technology cannot—that a dog can help that person regain mobility and independence and can help that person get his or her life back—then that is the beauty of his organization.

"Our primary purpose, our number-one purpose," says Stovroff, "is helping the veterans. I've been through combat. I know what these men and women are going through. Cash is everything to me. He's always by my side. All you need to do is look into a dog's eyes. That love never disappears. It's always there."

Stovroff with Cash and therapy dog Jenny.

Stovroff's is just one of the many lives changed by a trained service dog.

RENEE CHAMPAGNE
&
MILEY

You need to get your military bearing together.

~ Nurse case manager, Landstuhl
Regional Medical Center

enee Olshan Champagne had been calling every humane society and rescue
organization in the Williamsburg, Virginia, area. "I was devastated at the loss of my
dog Sadie," says Champagne, an Air Force veteran who was struggling with post-
traumatic stress and a TBI. "I reached out to everyone. I called all of the shelters and
explained that I needed a dog."

Why dogs have such a powerful effect on people remains a bit of mystery. What makes
for such a strong human–canine attraction? Why are some dogs and owners fully in
sync with each other from day one? Plenty of research indicates that the human–canine
relationship is not one-sided, either. Although the final puzzle pieces—the whys and
hows—have yet to be put into place, ongoing research is getting us much closer to the
answers.

"God was looking out for me that day," says Champagne, who believes that reasons—
unexplainable reasons that go beyond mere coincidence—exist as to why Miley was put
in her path. "How was it that she was there—at the shelter—on the day I called?"

Renee noticed Miley's inner and outer beauty right away.

The three-year-old Golden Retriever, with possibly a pinch of Labrador Retriever milling about in her DNA, had been surrendered by her owner to the Heritage Humane Society in Williamsburg, Virginia, on the very day that Champagne called searching for a dog. The shelter knew very few details about Miley's history, only that she had originally come from a breeder and had been surrendered to the shelter because the owner's child was allergic to her.

By the time Champagne arrived at the shelter on that September day in 2013, several other potential adopters had already shown interest in Miley. This was no surprise, considering that Miley is remarkably gorgeous, full of instinct, and overflowing with personality. "I connected with her immediately," says Champagne.

The shelter required a holding period, ranging from a few days to a week, for veterinary and behavioral evaluations. Miley wasn't going anywhere for a few days. "I went back every day to be with her, and we've been together ever since. I saved her, but she ended up saving me," says Champagne.

Joining the United States Air Force in 1996, Champagne attended six weeks of basic training and another twelve weeks of Security Forces training. "I loved that job," says Champagne. "I loved everything about it."

Two years into her service, Champagne was drugged and raped while on a training exercise; this resulted in a TBI, leaving her cognitively affected on the right side with short- and long-term memory loss and processing difficulties. Burying the assault memories for years, Champagne sensed that something was wrong, but she didn't know what.

Before Miley, there was Sadie, a two-year-old Golden Retriever mix who Champagne and her husband, a USAF colonel, had adopted from a North Carolina Golden Retriever rescue organization. Sadie was not specifically trained as a service dog—and Champagne didn't even know that she needed a service dog at that time—but Champagne and Sadie bonded instantly. "I knew the minute I saw her that she was the dog for me."

Sadie's Golden Retriever ancestry made her eager to give and receive affection, and Sadie became Champagne's canine first responder. Their strong human–canine relationship fostered Sadie's natural canine instincts, allowing her to sense Champagne's anxiety and stress levels and act accordingly—tapping or hugging Champagne to calm her and bring her back to the present.

Judy Bordignon is the force behind the Sirius K9 Service Dogs and Training Center, the organization that trained Miley and matched her with Renee.

After several years and assignments, Champagne transferred to Germany with her husband. An avid athlete and wellness coordinator, Champagne became the host of a healthy-living show in Germany, but she admitted that she wasn't dealing with day-to-day issues. By 2002, she had two children and had moved on to a civilian life. Yet she still could not pinpoint the cause of anxiety that encircled her life. "I went from running marathons to not being able to do a push up," says Champagne. "Never in my life have I not completed anything. I left the military feeling incomplete."

In 2012, an incident triggered memories of the 1998 sexual trauma that Champagne had buried years prior. A trigger can be any sight, sound, smell, or event that prompts a memory that can be associated with a prior trauma or significant amount of distress. Diagnosed with delayed-onset PTSD, she sought counseling and underwent prolonged exposure therapy—the military's standard treatment for PTSD—to deal with the invisible wounds and long-term effects associated with PTSD. Exposure therapy exposes individuals to extended amounts of time revisiting traumatic memories in detail, remembering the smells, sights, sounds, and thoughts that occurred at the time of the event. The point is for the person to revisit the memory again and again until the anxiety associated with it diminishes.

Only during this therapy did Champagne begin to remember and understand that the 1998 rape—now termed *military sexual assault* (MST) by the VA—was the reason for the deep emotional wounds, nightmares, stress, anxiety, headaches, and flashbacks and her inability to psychologically move beyond the trauma. The VA also prescribed antianxiety and antidepressant medications, which, according to Champagne, only worsened her PTSD symptoms.

Miley has the confident, stable temperament that's essential for performing her duties in public.

During Champagne's PTSD treatment at Germany's Landstuhl Regional Medical Center, Sadie, who had fulfilled Champagne's need to heal by providing immeasurable comfort; who on countless occasions had quieted Champagne's anxiety, frustration, and sadness with a simple touch or hug; and who had provided unconditional love during those difficult years simply by being there, passed away. "I was in a very dark place during that time," says Champagne, "and the loss of one of my principle sources of comfort did not help my situation."

Returning stateside without Sadie, Champagne desperately needed a faithful companion, which brought her to that fateful day when she and Miley crossed paths. "I was drowning, and she was my life jacket," says Champagne.

When Champagne's friend, retired Lt. Col. Kathy Champion (see page 160), heard about Miley, she encouraged Champagne to become the first veteran to receive a trained dog through the newly created Sirius K9 Service Dogs and Training Center, founded by Judy Bordignon in November 2013. As a Sirius K9 board member

Miley lies quietly under Renee's chair during lunch with a friend.

since its inception, Champion assists with public education and obtaining sponsorships for the training of service dogs for veterans. Dogs are donated at no cost to the veterans or the organization, but the cost of training ranges between $5,000 and $10,000 per dog, depending on whether the veteran is participating in the owner-trained service-dog group or the dog is acquired, trained, and donated by Bordignon's organization. Those expenses are mitigated by donor sponsors who cover the cost of the training materials, harnesses, vests, and any required travel associated with training, as well as follow-up support for the life of that veteran–service-dog team.

Sirius K9 Service Dogs and Training Center, a 501(c)(3) nonprofit in St. Petersburg, Florida, differs from other organizations that train service dogs in that Bordignon will evaluate the veteran's current dog, whether purebred or mixed-breed, shelter or rescue, small or large, to assess his temperament and whether or not he can handle the training necessary for service-dog work. Regardless of breed, a service dog requires a sound and social temperament to manage any fallout from the owner's PTSD. He needs a calm demeanor so that he won't overreact in public, bolt at strange sounds, chase after children playing, or become distracted by other animals. He needs to stay focused and not run off to follow birds or retrieve a stick should the owner accidentally drop the leash or harness.

About nine months had passed between the day that Champagne brought Miley home from the shelter and Bordignon's visit to Champagne's Virginia home to assess Miley's qualifications as a service dog and to conduct some preliminary training.

"Miley was bomb-proof," says Bordignon, a certified professional trainer (CPT) and former Southeastern Guide Dogs trainer. Although Miley may not have been a purebred Golden Retriever, she had inherited the breed's characteristically quiet, calm, intelligent, biddable, rock-solid temperament. For decades, these traits have defined the breed's ancestors as useful, versatile, working gun dogs capable of finding and retrieving game, both feathered and furred. Miley's high level of sociability toward people and her willingness to learn and remember her training are key qualities that trainers look for in service dogs.

"Miley surfaced as one of the best service-dog candidates I have ever assessed," says Bordignon. "Her obedience was exceptional and already secure, and she naturally demonstrated many of the tasks that would be required of a service dog, including exceptional poise and confidence in the public arena."

By the end of the week-long assessment, Bordignon approved her for training. In June 2014, Miley flew with Bordignon back to Florida, where Miley completed a ten-week training program that would fortify her service-dog skills. Normally, service-dog training takes anywhere from six months to one year or longer because dogs learn bonding, social interactions, obedience training, and more. Because of the preexisting bond between Champagne and Miley, as well as Miley's advanced obedience skills at the time of her adoption, she required less formal training than is typically necessary.

Later that summer, Champagne drove to Florida, and she and Miley underwent two weeks of extensive training with Bordignon. The normal training period is longer, but, again, due to Miley's advanced skills and the strong bond between Champagne and Miley, she required less extensive training.

Champagne had to learn how to handle Miley as well as how to handle herself with Miley. She needed to learn how to get the dog to *sit*, *down*, *stay*, and *move*; how to get Miley into an elevator and turned around; how to give commands; and how to use Miley when she was feeling anxious. "It was a very difficult time," explains Champagne.

"I felt disabled. Kathy and Judy were so patient, but there was so much training. It was exhausting. And I hated using the dog's harness. I was more comfortable using a leash."

She admits that, in the beginning, using Miley's green service vest with the "Please Don't Touch Me—I'm Working" patch was difficult, too. "I used to be embarrassed about having a service dog. I didn't want people to know I needed one," says Champagne. Because people can't see her psychological wounds, they never fully understand the human–canine relationship, the impenetrable bond between Champagne and Miley. Subsequently, they ask inappropriate questions: "What's wrong with you?" "Why do you need a service dog? You don't look disabled." "What happened?" Some even go as far as to make statements like, "For a veteran, you're doing really well."

Miley is specifically trained to mitigate the effects of PTSD, which includes sensing anxiety in Champagne before it turns into a full-blown panic attack. By pawing, nudging, hugging, or even jumping on Champagne, Miley quiets Champagne's mind, pulling her back to the present. This calming effect was evident during a court appearance in which Champagne testified, reliving the trauma of her sexual assault. On the witness stand next to Champagne lay Miley, monitoring her owner's breathing, scrutinizing her body language. On several occasions, Miley laid a paw on Champagne to calm her. Locking eyes, Miley let her know, *I'm here for you.* Even in her agitated state, Champagne couldn't help but smile and pet Miley. Doing so calmed her and brought her out of the past and back to the present.

"It was so hard, and I didn't want anyone patting me on the back or asking, 'Are you OK?'" explains Champagne. "I was so alone. I had no energy to do anything. It took so much energy to work on myself, but Miley's just being there was enough. It takes no work, no energy to be with Miley. She's never going to hurt me. She's just there. She's quiet. I don't feel guilty. I don't need to talk or explain myself."

In addition to *hug*, Miley understands twenty-six commands, including basic obedience commands. She is trained to *block*, which is a standard behavior for PTSD-trained dogs and is designed to create a barrier between Champagne and other people. Miley also turns and faces *back* to watch Champagne's back, and she will immediately alert if something is not right.

Furthermore, Champagne's TBI affected the parts of the brain that govern vision, balance, and learning. Subsequently, Miley is also a balance dog, with her harness serving as a brace or counterbalance to assist Champagne.

Some days, Champagne thinks she is doing OK, yet Miley senses her increased stress and anxiety, and she takes over. "She'll jump on the bed and lie down next to me," says

Miley accompanies Renee as she tries on clothes in a store's dressing room.

Champagne. "One day, recently, I was in a bad state, but I felt safe with Miley lying next to me. With Miley, I don't have to medicate myself during difficult times. Her love is more powerful than any medication or alcohol."

Miley is saving Champagne's life just as Champagne saved hers two years ago. Because of Miley, Champagne has a renewed sense of confidence and has returned to her athletic roots as an avid yoga instructor and endurance runner. With Miley by her side, she's also attending graduate school, where she is fulfilling the requirements for a master's degree in clinical mental health at the College of William and Mary.

After graduation, Champagne plans to specialize in helping military families struggling with PTSD. "PTSD is a family diagnosis," says Champagne. "It affects everyone in the family." No doubt Miley will play a pivotal role in helping those families, just as she helps Champagne and her family.

Champagne also is researching post-traumatic growth—referring to positive psychological changes as the result of dealing with adversity—as a response to military stressors. She believes that having a service dog can help foster post-traumatic growth not only with the veteran but also with the veteran's family.

Life for Miley is not all work and no play. "Unless I need her, she's a family dog," explains Champagne. "But she transforms from a family dog to my service dog in an instant." True to her Golden Retriever background, Miley has an innate love of life. She's goofy and lovable and loves playing soccer, swimming, retrieving, and running with Champagne. In addition to her important work as Champagne's partner and protector, Miley fills Champagne's life with endless unconditional love, comfort, and support. "She makes all of us laugh, but when the vest goes on, she's a completely different dog. It's all about the work when the vest goes on."

TED MARTELLO
&
BUSTER

A dog is the only thing on earth that loves
you more than he loves himself.

~ Josh Billings

All smiles and exuding uncontrollable tail wags, Chow Chow mix Buster was picked up on the side of a highway in 2012. How long the mixed-breed dog had been roaming the streets is anyone's guess. With no identification—no collar, no tag, no microchip—Buster was turned over to the Best Friends Animal Sanctuary 5 miles north of Kanab, in Utah's Angel Canyon.

Home to nearly 2,000 homeless animals, from dogs and cats to birds, rabbits, horses, goats, mules, and even pigs, Buster quickly caught the eye of Sherry Woodard, the sanctuary's animal-behavior expert who teaches dog trainers and rescue groups as well as sheriff's department personnel and prison staff how to identify, screen, select, train, and place appropriate shelter and rescue dogs for career work.

It was love at first sight for Ted, who knew that Buster was the dog for him after just seeing his photograph.

"Buster has a love of life that shows all the time," says Woodard. "He smiles and wags more than many dogs. I knew that would be helpful to give his person a sense of happy every day." From day one, Woodard noticed that Buster was very interactive, and his focus on her was quick to emerge; she saw this as an ability to quickly bond with a new owner. Equally impressive was Buster's empathy—his seemingly innate ability to identify and understand a person's situation and feelings.

Whether or not dogs feel empathy is an ongoing debate, with expert psychologists, behavioral biologists, researchers, and dog trainers arguing both sides of the issue. Some suggest that it's not empathy but rather emotional contagion—meaning that the dog is responding to the emotions of a person without fully understanding what the person is feeling (empathizing). However you classify Buster's behavior, it would prove to be beneficial in his new service-dog job.

Twice deployed to Iraq, Army E-4 Specialist Ted Martello left the military in 2013 after being injured by an IED on his second tour. Struggling with PTSD and a TBI, Martello, who works for Catholic Charities to help other disabled veterans find housing, went in search of a service dog. At a Las Vegas Stand Down event (a national

Buster and Ted at the airport. Service dogs are typically allowed to board planes with their owners.

grassroots, community-based intervention program designed to help the nation's estimated 60,000 homeless veterans combat life on the streets), Martello heard about Canines with Careers—run by Woodard—that places rescued canines in jobs, which saves the dogs' lives and, in turn, benefits people.

"After contacting Woodard and explaining my situation," says Martello, "she sent me photos and descriptions of three dogs, and I knew Buster was the one for me. There was something about his eyes. His face."

On Memorial Day weekend 2012, Martello made the drive from his Arizona home to Utah, where he met his future service dog, Buster. Buster and Martello formed an instant bond, and they have been together ever since.

Buster and Martello spent a year working with Karen London, Ph.D., a certified applied animal behaviorist (CAAB) in Flagstaff, Arizona, instilling basic obedience commands and teaching Buster how to behave appropriately in all types of situations, including on public transportation (taxis, buses, airplanes, trains), in restaurants, in stores, in elevators, in crowds, around noises, and amid other distractions. Buster's training also includes mitigating behaviors specific to Martello's PTSD, which is designed to provide Martello with emotional support as well as more independence, freedom, and positive interaction.

Unlike selectively bred service dogs, Buster was not bred to impress. His background lacks the generations of parents, grandsires, and granddams selectively bred for service-dog work. In fact, his history is unknown, and it's highly unlikely that it contains any links to the popular breeds—the Labrador Retriever and the Golden Retriever—most noted for service-dog work. However, Buster's ace in the hole is his absolute devotion to Martello. He's Martello's best friend and companion. His battle buddy.

How and why Buster ended up alone on the side of a highway is unclear. Had his life been all about staying alive? Foraging in trash cans? Had he, at one time, been someone's cherished pet? Had he escaped through a gate inadvertently left open? Had he wandered away from home? Had he been betrayed by humans— dumped or abandoned on the side of a road, a common practice among badly misinformed owners?

"Buster has some great traits," says London. "He's super agreeable, comfortable with different situations, and not easily distracted. He adores Ted. He's very connected with Ted, and he looks to Ted for information." Equally important, London adds, is that Buster has a natural ability to be attuned to his environment, to scan what is going on around him, and to alert Martello. "It's difficult to train a dog without that

The pilot snaps a photo of this amazing twosome.

Buster is by Ted's side wherever he goes.

skill. I love working with this pair—it's as good as it gets. And Ted just seems to be happier all the time."

Buster's weakness, if one can call it that, is his high sociability with other dogs. "The only time he broke service was to play with another dog," says Martello. A serious breach of professional duty, but Martello doesn't hold it against him. Rather, he takes a proactive approach, asking Buster to sit when other dogs are approaching or playing nearby. "We just could not train that out of him. He's better now, but he's still very social with other dogs."

Like thousands of veterans struggling with PTSD and TBIs, Martello, who spent thirteen years in the Army, isolated himself, leaving his home only to go to work because being in or around crowds was too overwhelming. Today, Martello relies on

Buster to gauge the safety of his surroundings, which allows him to venture into public without constantly worrying about people crowding too close. Trained to *block*, Buster keeps people from getting too close to Martello. He also alerts Martello when someone is approaching from behind.

Trained to recognize when Martello's breathing changes or his pulse quickens, Buster will paw, nudge, bump, or otherwise distract Martello to interrupt his anxiety before it turns into a full-blown panic attack. He also performs these behaviors to interrupt Martello's nightmares. "If I get upset," says Martello, "he calms me down by nudging my hand, which distracts me enough to stop the bad feelings."

Through a strong human–canine bond and appropriate, specialized training, Buster has restored Martello's confidence and independence. A passionate advocate for veterans, Martello now speaks publicly for Best Friends Animal Sanctuary about the benefits of service dogs and how Buster changed his life. "Because I have to walk him," explains Martello, "it helps me get out in public, interact with people." He adds that everybody in his town knows Buster, and they always want to pet him, which provides additional opportunities for Martello to raise awareness about service dogs for wounded veterans. Whether he is speaking to hundreds of veterans or a few people in his hometown who have stopped to meet Buster, Martello is passionate about service dogs and helping other veterans. "Without Buster, I wouldn't be here. It's that simple," says Martello.

8

HOW DOGS
READ US

HOW DOGS READ US

A lot of controversy exists about whether or not dogs can be trained to predict seizures, or, as is the case with several of the veterans profiled in this book, migraines or heart arrhythmias. Most trainers will tell you that dogs can't be trained to predict impending seizures. Rather, they are trained to respond to the most minute changes in a person's deportment and possibly scent cues, which may be triggered in a person as a result of a seizure.

Despite the lack of scientific evidence, plenty of dogs appear to have figured out on their own how to foretell an impending seizure, migraine, arrhythmia, or even nightmare. But how?

It's clear that dogs are experts at decoding body language (far more adept than most humans are at reading canine body language). After all, interpreting body language is a dog's specialized communication system. It's how they survived long before they were domesticated and how they connect with humans today. So in tune are dogs at reading body language that they can detect tiny microchanges in a person's posture, facial expression, or breathing patterns before the person knows that he or she is giving off the signal. These changes are so minute that they're imperceptible to human eyes.

Realizing exactly how perceptive dogs are is often lost on many people. Equally important, most owners do not even realize that they're signaling the dog. A horse named Clever Hans, however, may help to illustrate the nonverbal messages that owners send—and dogs receive.

At the turn of the twentieth century, Clever Hans was a world-famous German horse whose owner, Wilhelm von Osten, thought that Hans could count—as well as tell time, read, and spell (in German, of course!). Von Osten would ask Hans questions like "What's seven and five?" and Hans would tap or stamp his foot twelve times. Hans could even tap out the answers to questions like "What is the square root of sixteen?" or "If the eighth day of the month comes on Tuesday, what is the date for the following Friday?" He also would use his nose to indicate which kerchief was red, green, or yellow. Thousands of people on both sides of the Atlantic observed Hans, and

Dogs and owners often develop a special bond that enables them to tune in to each other's body language, moods, and feelings.

although many believed trickery was involved, no one was ever able to produce the slightest evidence.

Eventually, a psychologist named Oskar Pfungst debunked the mystery surrounding Hans's mathematical abilities and proved that he wasn't really counting. Through close observation, Pfungst realized that Hans was responding to unconscious cues from his trainer or, in some instances, other questioners; this phenomenon later became known as the "Clever Hans effect." These extremely slight changes in posture or facial expression cued Hans when to start and stop tapping his foot. So subtle, so minute were the cues that even Pfungst couldn't see them—and he was looking for them.

The mystery was solved when Pfungst put von Osten (and other questioners) out of view and had them put questions to Hans that even they didn't know the answers to. It turns out that Hans could answer almost all of the questions correctly—regardless of who the questioners were—as long as the questioners already knew the answers and were visible to Hans. Absent either of those conditions, Hans's proficiency plummeted.

Obviously, Hans was clever. He was rewarded for correct behaviors, which, in turn, reinforced those behaviors. Although he didn't possess the intelligence to count or learn mathematics or even color identification, his level of awareness was astonishing, and his story helps illustrate behaviors that he acquired without the help of humans.

Similarly, experts say that dogs can't be trained to predict seizures; rather, like Hans, they are so extraordinarily astute at reading and responding to the subtlest changes in their owners' expressions, gestures, postures, respirations, and temperatures that it allows some dogs to learn on their own to identify signs that predict the onset of a seizure. This is not unlike the behavior of nightmare interruption, which, again, trainers say can't be trained but is a behavior that some dogs have learned on their own as a result of a strong human–canine bond.

If that's the case, how is it possible that Carolyn Jette's service dog Troy (see page 222) was able to "alert" her on his first night home with her that she was about to have a seizure? How was Kent Phyfe's new service dog, Mike, able to alert him to a heart arrhythmia the very first night as well?

In her book, *Animals in Translation, Using the Mysteries of Autism to Decode Animal Behavior*, author Temple Grandin writes, "It's one thing for a dog to start recognizing the signs that a seizure is coming; you might chalk that up to unique aspects of canine hearing, smell, or vision, like the fact that a dog can hear a dog whistle while a human can't. But it's another thing for a dog to start to recognize the signs of an impending seizure and then decide to do something about it. That's what intelligence is in humans; intelligence in people using their built-in perceptual and cognitive skills to achieve useful and sometimes remarkable goals."

Research presented by John J. Ensminger in his 2010 book *Service and Therapy Dogs in American Society* suggests that alerting behavior is not breed-, age-, or gender-specific, but that the effectiveness of an alerting dog "depends greatly upon the human companion to recognize and respond appropriately to the dog's alerting behavior."

A 2012 online study done by Dawn A. Marcus and Amrita Phowmick surveyed 1,029 adult migraineurs and found that 54 percent of the participants identified a change in their dog's behavior that might be used as a predictor of an impending migraine. Nearly 60 percent of the participants indicated that their dogs had alerted them to the onset of a headache, usually an hour or two in advance.

The most common alerting behavior was the dog's refusal to leave his owner (i.e., a "Velcro dog"). Other alerting

Service dogs can come in any size or shape.

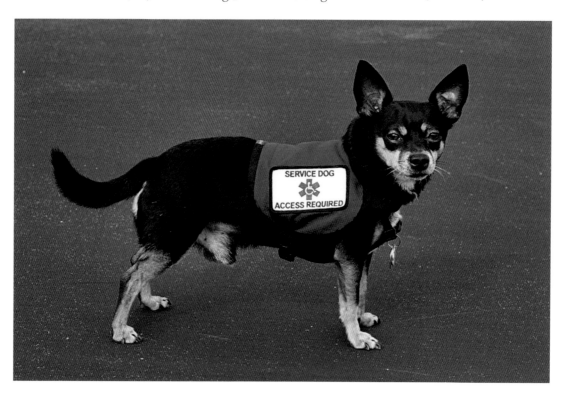

behaviors included excessive or persistent licking, sitting or lying on the owner, sitting close and staring at the owner, restricting the person's usual activity level, and "herding" the owner to a couch or bed. One owner reported that her dog would bark, wag his tail frantically, and whirl in circles starting an hour or two before the onset of a migraine. Nearly 58 percent of the owners were able to identify the dog's alerting behavior before symptoms of a migraine attack typically began.

But what about the owner who says that his or her dog wasn't in the same room but suddenly ran into the room to alert? Research suggests that we must consider signals independent of visual cues, such as the possibility of a scent or auditory cue.

Research shows us that a dog's olfactory skills are truly astounding. Some experts estimate that dogs can smell 10,000 to 100,000 times better than humans can. Others say dogs smell at a DNA level. According to Brent A. Craven et al.'s article "The Fluid Dynamics of Canine Olfaction" in the June 2010 issue of the scientific journal *Interface*, dogs can detect some odors in parts per trillion—as in odor concentration levels at one to two parts per trillion. In her book *Inside of a Dog: What Dogs See, Smell, and Know*, Alexandra Horowitz writes that while we might notice if our cup of coffee has a teaspoon of sugar added to it, a dog can detect a teaspoon of sugar in a million gallons of water (equivalent to two Olympic-sized pools!). James Walker, former director of the Sensory Research Institute at Florida State University, is quoted in Peter Tyson's article "Dogs' Dazzling Sense of Smell" written for *NOVA scienceNOW*, as saying: "If you make the analogy to vision, what you and I can see at one third of a mile, a dog could see more than 3,000 miles away and still see as well."

What do dogs' noses have that humans' don't? For starters, dogs possess up to 300 million olfactory, or scent, receptors in their noses, compared to about six million for humans. And, most remarkably, the part of a dog's brain that is devoted to analyzing smells is—in proportional terms—about forty times greater than the comparable area in humans' brains.

A dog's nose also functions differently than a human's does. Bloodhounds are known as the world champions of canine sniffing. Capable of catching a scent on the ground hours or even days after the source has passed through, Bloodhounds have more nose tissue—basically, more nose—than many breeds, and they have long pendulum-style ears that fall close to the head and fan up more scented air for the nose to catch. A Bloodhound can come to a fork in the road, a stream, or a patch of grass in an open field and determine, *I think Suzy went this way*. This is a remarkable feat, considering that the dog is also dealing with changes in wind direction, changes in speed, humidity, and most likely a potpourri of other scents, including soil, water, grasses, animal droppings, and even human scents.

Here's what is also fascinating: when humans inhale, the odorous air goes in and comes back out the same way, and our sense of smell is relegated to a small region on the roof of the nasal cavity. Dogs, on the other hand, have a nasal structure that allows them to separate the air they breathe into distinct flow paths, with a percentage of the scented air—estimated to be about 12 or 13 percent—detouring to a recessed area in the back of the nose that is dedicated to olfaction. The remaining air—the respiratory air—sweeps past this area and into the lungs.

Once the scented air enters the olfactory recess, it filters through a web of scroll-like bony structures called *turbinates*, which contain specialized nerve cells that feed sensory information concerning smells to the dog's brain.

Also, humans have two nasal passages, so when they exhale through their noses, they send the air, along with any odors, out. Dogs, in contrast, have four nasal passages, two inner passages and two on the outside. The inner canals pull in the scented air and then exhale to the outer canals in such a way that the exhaling air doesn't disturb the new incoming odors.

Unlike humans, dogs can also determine which nostril an odor arrived in, which helps in their ability to locate the source of smells. (Dogs do breathe through their mouths, but they're not using it for scenting. Dogs don't sweat, so they cool themselves by panting through their mouths.)

The canine nose is a complex and efficient organ.

Dogs also have a vomeronasal organ, known as the Jacobson's organ, that sits above the roof (hard palate) of the mouth, along the floor of the nose, or nasal septum. In dogs, the receptor sites are covered in cilia, allowing dogs to pick up pheromones, which are the naturally produced chemicals that tend to cause a reaction from other members of the same species. Some pheromones trigger an action when danger is present, while others are sexual in nature. Because the vomeronasal organ is recessed inside the nose, it's hard for odors to land on it. As a result, the pheromone odors don't get mixed up with the brain's analysis of other odors. So where is all of this going?

We know that trainers have been able to harness a dog's natural scenting ability to sniff out drugs and explosives, such as IEDs along the road, and even to track lost children or hunt down insurgents. Imprinting an odor is how dogs learn to seek out bombs, weapons, drugs, humans, and even human remains, yet little scientific data exist about whether dogs can smell our emotions. Some experienced dog trainers and handlers, including some from search-and-rescue and law enforcement, will tell you that they believe dogs can distinguish people who are in a high state of fear or arousal just based on their scent. Are the dogs actually smelling fear or simply reading microshifts in body language—not unlike Clever Hans?

Interestingly, Kevin Behan, author of the 2012 book *Your Dog Is Your Mirror*, describes how he believes that various police dogs appear to sense criminal intent in some people before they actually commit a crime. This is an ability that stems from a solid human–canine bond between the dog and his handler—a bond that runs so deep that the author calls it "fusion," in which the dog "perceives himself in the handler." This megabond between dog and handler is what allows some dogs to sense danger before something actually happens, so it's plausible that this is also what allows some dogs to detect and "alert" to migraines, heart arrhythmias, or seizures in advance of their occurrence.

A person's emotional state has a profound impact on his or her dog, and, considering a dog's super-sniffing capabilities and absent scientific data, it seems reasonable that dogs can "smell" changes in our emotions relatively easily. Do a person's emotions or odor change before he or she experiences an epileptic seizure, migraine, or heart arrhythmia? Could dogs be picking up on stress or an impending seizure not only through movement but also through smell?

In addition to having excellent sniffers, dogs also see pretty well, too—despite certain misconceptions. One mistaken belief is that dogs are color blind—meaning that they see only shades of gray. Special light-catching cells called *cones* allow dogs and humans to see color. Humans have three different types of cones, and the combined activity of these cones is why humans (unless they're color blind) have a full range of color vision. Dogs have only two kinds of cones, so while they do see color, they see fewer colors than do humans.

The simple question of how well dogs see is, well, pretty complicated, but it's safe to say that dogs probably see the world differently than do humans (or cats, horses, goats, or birds of prey). Most typically, a dog's visual acuity (the ability to clearly see the tiny details of what he's looking at) is about 20/75, meaning that a dog's quality of vision at 20 feet away from an object is comparable to a person's quality of vision at 75 feet away from the object. In other words, the dog has to get much closer to an object than a human does to see it clearly.

Obviously, visual acuity varies from breed to breed, but this helps to explain why some dogs don't see a tidbit of kibble on the floor even when it's right under their noses—even when you're pointing and saying, "It's right there!" Unless they

Dogs can be trained to use their super sniffers to detect drugs and other contraband.

Dogs use all of their senses to detect minute changes in the people with whom they've bonded closely.

saw the kibble drop, they aren't likely to see it, but they're probably able to smell it!

Basically, canine genetics have allowed dogs to trade good visual acuity for good nighttime vision, and here's why: Dogs and humans use *rods* (photoreceptors) to see in dim light, but dogs have more rods in the center of the retina. In people, the center of the retina has more cones, which are important for color vision and vision in bright light. Also, a dog's superiorly located reflective *tapetum lucidum*—the part of the eye that acts as a mirror, reflecting light—enhances his ability to detect objects in dim light by reflecting light back through the retina a second time and providing the photoreceptors at least two chances at capturing each quantum of light. (The mirror effect of the tapetum is the "eye shine" you see in a dog's eyes at night.) Although dim light is enhanced by the tapetum, it may also result in less acuity.

Those dominant photoreceptors in dogs—the rods—allow dogs to see moving objects and shapes better than stationary ones. A 1936 study of the visual performance of fourteen police dogs was cited in a 1995 article titled "Vision in Dogs" by Paul E. Miller and Christopher J. Murphy for the *Journal of the American Veterinary Medical Association*. The study showed that the "most sensitive dogs could recognize moving objects at a distance of 810 to 900 meters but could recognize the same object, when stationary, at a distance of only 585 meters or less. "

How a dog's eyes are set in his head determines his field of vision, with eye set varying by breed. Although a human's eyes are set straight forward, a dog's eyes (again, depending on the breed) are usually set at 20-degree angles, thus providing a more encompassing field of view (the area that can be seen by an eye when it is fixed on one point) of 250–270 degrees, which is greater than humans' field of vision, which is about 180 degrees.

A service dog, who spends most, if not all, of his time with his owner, becomes very proficient at reading the person's almost imperceptible cues.

Using Their Senses

Like humans, dogs use sight, sound, smell, taste, and touch to explore and interpret the world around them, which may help to explain, in part, why it's possible for dogs who don't speak our language to possess the uncanny ability to read us like, well, a book.

While a dog's overall visual acuity is weaker than a human's, the dog's slightly angled eye set allows a greater field of vision.

Most interestingly, an international collaboration led by scientists from Trinity College Dublin, Ireland, as well as researchers from the University of Edinburgh and the University of St. Andrews, Scotland, has shown that dogs can take in visual information 25 percent faster than a human can. Yet they see movements almost as if in slow motion, which may help explain why dogs are so adept at picking up minute movements and gestures that are invisible to the human eye.

Like a dog's sense of smell, his sense of hearing is also superior to that of humans. Without delving into the hertz and kilohertz ranges, it's safe to say that dogs hear at a wider range of frequencies than do humans. In other words, they hear pretty much everything we hear and then some. Again, much depends on the dog's breed, age, and ear size and shape, with many dogs hearing at a distance up to four times farther than humans.

Revolutionary Bonds

History is chock full of stories of the human–canine bond, many of them about military men and their profound friendships with their canine companions. Consider that General George Washington, who had a love of hounds and terriers, made a point during the American Revolutionary War of returning British General William Howe's Fox Terrier in October 1777, after the little dog had apparently lost his way during the battle and had fallen in with American troops as they marched north.

Several versions of the story exist, and although it's impossible to know with absolute certainty what transpired, Caroline Tiger writes in her book, *General Howe's Dog*, that when one of Washington's officers suggested keeping the dog as a mascot, Washington demurred. Washington, a dog lover himself, would "no doubt have had empathy for the sadness a man might feel over the loss of a pet." Perhaps Washington had a particular compassion for the little Fox Terrier because he had many terriers and hunting hounds at his Mount Vernon home.

After cleaning up the dog, brushing his fur, and giving him some food, Washington, according to Tiger, asked his aide-de-camp Alexander Hamilton to pen a note to Howe, which read,

General Washington's compliments to General Howe, does himself the pleasure to return him a Dog, which accidentally fell into his hands, and by inscription on the collar, appears to belong to General Howe.

One of Washington's men backtracked the 25 miles to Germantown, where Howe was headquartered, and returned the dog.

Research keeps taking us back to the human–canine relationship. The "megabond" we talked about earlier allows dogs to acquire and perform behaviors without the help of humans—just like Clever Hans. It's a human–canine relationship that is so solid and so profound that it allows dogs to respond to the subtlest changes in their owners' behavior.

Setting aside the scientific aspect of how human–canine bonding came about, how is it possible that the presence of a dog in a person's life can generate humanity and compassion and a nearly impenetrable bond? How is it possible that the mere presence of a 70-pound Labrador Retriever can inspire a 6-foot-3 inch, 255-pound combat soldier? How does the touch of a Golden Retriever instantly wash away the stress and anxiety of a third-generation combat Marine? How does the sight of a mixed-breed rescued from a high-kill animal shelter save the life of a veteran teetering on the brink of suicide?

Maybe part of it can be chalked up to oxytocin—the "feel-good hormone" that is associated with social bonding. Then again, maybe it has nothing to do with science and everything to do with a dog's innate ability to bring out the best in some people.

Despite mounds of scientific data, including canine brain imaging results that show us that dogs have mental processes similar to our own, the human–canine bond is quite inexplicable at times. Why humans love dogs so much, and why and how dogs reciprocate those feelings with unconditional, nonjudgmental companionship is perfectly complementary. Whether dogs are alerting or responding to seizures, interrupting nightmares, or de-escalating stressful situations, it is that megabond, the simple yet complex human–canine relationship that so many speak about, that has saved injured veterans during their darkest hours more than any human being could have. To love a dog and to be loved unconditionally in return. Is it really that simple?

Proof of the connection between soldiers and dogs dates back to the days of George Washington.

CAROLYN JETTE
&
TROY

A good navy is not a provocation to war.
It is the surest guaranty of peace.

~ President Theodore Roosevelt,
December 2, 1902, second annual message to Congress

Epilepsy ended Carolyn Jette's military career, but a Labrador Retriever named Troy saved her life and gave her a second chance at a brighter future.

Jette's naval career began at Naval Station Great Lakes, located on the southwestern shore of Lake Michigan in Illinois. This training center has been in use since 1911, with President Theodore Roosevelt presiding over its beginnings. Yet, Jette's dream of becoming a naval officer ended in San Diego, California—3,000 miles from her Massachusetts home—seven months after enlisting in the United States Navy in February 1996.

Two months shy of completing radioman training, eighteen-year-old Jette had a seizure—her first ever. "I don't remember much," says Jette. "I woke up in the emergency room."

Troy has enabled Carolyn to be involved in her children's school and activities.

At first, doctors couldn't find anything wrong, and she returned to duty. Two weeks later, another seizure and another trip to the hospital. That's when doctors began the medical tests that would eventually diagnose her with epilepsy.

Instead of being posted to a ship headed for Bosnia, Jette was deemed 30-percent disabled and medically discharged. She returned home to Massachusetts, heartbroken.

Growing up, Jette's lifelong love and passion was riding horses. Her family rode together, and she started competitive riding at a young age, continuing until she joined the Navy. Her diagnosis made riding a safety issue, but she continued riding, training, and giving lessons because other riders were always around to keep an eye on her. She married, and together she and her husband, a horse trainer, started their own business.

After the birth of her daughters, she continued to train and ride horses on her own, but her epilepsy grew increasingly worse. By 2000, her seizures had increased to around ten per day, and she was deemed 100-percent disabled. Driving was no longer an option.

Five years later, the seizures were so severe that they disrupted every aspect of her life. Her marriage ended, and she was forced to give up riding as well.

Stress, exhaustion, anxiety, depression, and poor diet can trigger seizures. As a single mom with two young daughters, disabled, and with no prospects for the future, Jette's life overflowed with triggers. Unable to work, go to school, support herself, or care for her daughters, she moved in with her parents.

Before Troy, Jette had no quality of life. "I couldn't even get off the couch," says Jette. As a result, in 2007, she opted for risky brain surgery. "The doctors told me that I could die on the table, wake up and not be able to speak, or wake up and be totally fine. I was willing to take the gamble. At that point, I had no quality of life."

Two hours after brain surgery, Jette was up and walking in the ICU. Following the surgery, her seizures decreased to six or seven per day. While she was grateful for fewer and less severe seizures, they continued disrupting her life.

Facing an uncertain future, she reached out to America's VetDogs (AVD) in Smithtown, New York. The process took nearly two years, but on June 21, 2009, Jette was partnered with Troy, a two-year-old yellow Labrador Retriever who is trained as a seizure-awareness or seizure-response dog. Together, they trained for one week at an off-campus AVD class in Maryland.

AVD trains dogs for seizure awareness—not anticipation or prediction. In other words, Troy is not trained to alert or predict seizures; rather, he is trained to respond to a seizure by retrieving Jette's car keys and cell phone, which has a medical pouch attached to it that contains her medication.

An epileptic seizure can't be stopped or interrupted once it starts. In an emergency, a doctor may use drugs to bring a lengthy seizure to an end. However, according to the Epilepsy Foundation of America, Inc., people can't do anything except wait for the seizure to run its course. This is why some seizure-response dogs are trained to lie on top of or beside the person having the seizure to prevent unintentional injury and/or to provide comfort when the person comes out of the seizure.

A lot of controversy still exists about whether a dog can be trained to predict a seizure before it starts (also known as a seizure-alert dog [SAD]), and, so far, experts say that

people haven't had a lot of luck trying. But a lot of dogs have figured it out on their own, writes animal-science expert Temple Grandin in her 2005 book *Animals in Translation: Using the Mysteries of Autism to Decode Animal Behavior.*

In Jette's case, she and Troy have formed such an amazing bond that he has come to recognize the signs of a seizure

ahead of time. No one really knows how Troy—or any dog—can predict seizures, but it happens. One 1998 study found that 10 percent of owners said that their seizure-response dogs had turned into seizure-alert dogs."

Such is the case with Troy who, according to Jette, is able to predict a seizure thirty minutes beforehand. Troy, who never barks, starts frantically barking, which alerts Jette and allows her to take seizure-control medication ahead of time. If Troy senses that Jette is about to experience a seizure during the night, he will nudge her or lick her face, which is enough to wake her and break the cycle before the seizure starts.

Seizure-free for five years, Jette was cleared to drive after six months. With Troy by her side, she returned to college and received her bachelor's degree in psychology, and she now works full-time for the state of Massachusetts. Her job requires her to drive about 100 miles per day, and, of course, Troy is by her side at all times.

Troy has given Jette the freedom, confidence, and ability to travel, too, and she has vacationed in both the United States and Mexico. (She and Troy were detained in Mexico City for a few hours—apparently, the authorities didn't quite understand the concept of service dogs.) She's also returned to her first love—riding. She rides at the Mini Prix level (the most exciting form of horse jumping, with fences approaching 6 feet in height) and competes for personal enjoyment.

"Anyone who has lived through the seizure aspect of my life," says Jette, "understands what Troy has done for me. I can never repay America's VetDogs. I couldn't function without him. He's my best friend. He's better than any medications. I have my life back, and my kids get to grow up with a mom because of Troy."

No definitive guidelines or mandatory age requirement exists for retiring a service dog. Jette anticipates that Troy, who was eight and a half years old at the time of writing, has about four years of service left. Before then—when he is around ten and a half— she plans to apply to AVD for a new seizure-response dog to ensure that she is never without a dog. "I'll never be able to replace Troy," says Jette, "but the decision is easier knowing that he will remain with us for the rest of his life."

JERRY BUSS & STORM

*Once you have a wonderful dog, a life
without one, is a life diminished.*

~Dean Koontz

Drafted in 1970, veteran Jerry Buss is one of 2.59 million American soldiers,
according to the Federal Register, who served in Vietnam. As an eighteen-year-
old US Army Indirect Fire Infantryman, Buss was a member of the combat
mortar platoon that was in charge of setting up, loading, and firing 60-mm, 81-mm,
and 120-mm combat mortars—the most powerful of any weapon in an infantry unit.
Returning stateside, he sought help for PTSD but was told by a doctor, "There's nothing
wrong with you, Jerry. Go away."

"I laugh about that now," says Buss, "but at the time, it wasn't very funny." For a
long time, Buss did not laugh much at all. He knew that something was wrong, but
he didn't know what. It would take another ten years before a private psychiatrist—
also a PTSD-affected Vietnam veteran—would diagnose Buss's issues. And yet
another thirty years before a service dog named Storm would free his captive mind
of recurring images and nightmares and help him deal with the long-term effects and
downward spiral of PTSD.

True to his breed, Storm is a friendly, energetic, and bright dog.

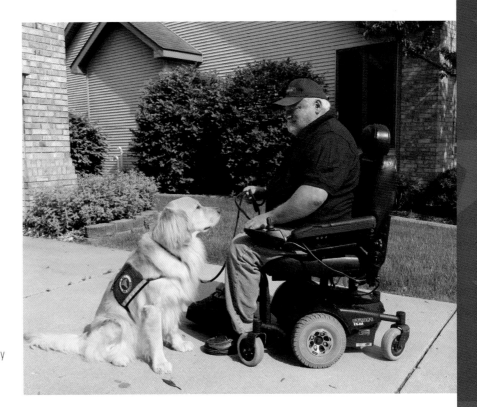

Storm provides Jerry not only with help in everyday tasks but also with the bond of companionship.

Storm helps Jerry, who is confined to a wheelchair, get around.

At the urging of his full-time private-duty nurse in 2013, Buss went in search of a service dog. Storm, a purebred Golden Retriever, was bred by a private breeder and then purchased, trained, matched, and donated to Buss in June 2014 by Veterans Moving Forward (VMF). The process from application to Storm's placement with Buss took about a year, but from then on, it's been one miracle after another.

"We tailor a dog's final training to the specific needs of the veteran," explains Karen Jeffries, the retired naval officer who founded VMF. "As time goes on, we learn that the dog is capable of doing more, and the veteran reveals more of his or her needs, never quite believing that the dog can do as much for him or her as is possible."

Before Storm, Buss, like thousands of veterans struggling with PTSD, isolated himself in his home and struggled with depression. Nightmares kept him up at night, and he teetered on the brink of suicide. It was as if his life had been lost for forty years someplace between Vietnam and a small town in Indiana.

Like so many tales of success, Storm, who is trained to mitigate the effects of PTSD, has become somewhat of a guiding light to Buss, restoring his will to live, keeping his life in motion. "When I first met Storm, I didn't know he was my dog," explains Buss.

"There were other dogs there, too, but Storm kept coming to me. I was elated when I found out he was going to be my dog." Buss knew that a service dog would change his life, but he didn't know how Storm would forever and completely change it for the better.

The first night with Storm, Buss slept for more than three hours—something he had not done in more years than he could count. It's not that he didn't want to sleep, but he dreaded the dreams and the uncertainty that almost always accompanied it. And he slept in his own bed, which was another huge turn of events.

Although Storm is not specifically trained to interrupt nightmares, it's a skill that most PTSD-trained service dogs develop on their own as a result of a strong human–canine bond. "If he needs to wake me, he nudges me with that big wet nose of his," says Buss. Yet the mere presence of Storm has reduced Buss's anxiety level immeasurably, which, in turn, has decreased the frequency of his nightmares.

Buss says, "I can now sleep through the night because I know if there's a problem, he will wake me up. Of course, he wouldn't hurt anyone, but I can sleep knowing he is there to let me know if there's an intruder."

While Buss still occasionally wrestles with his inner turmoil, he doesn't stay in the past for too long. Storm won't let him. Trained to detect when Buss is feeling anxious or experiencing a flashback, Storm will nudge him, nose-bump him, or lay his paw on Buss's lap, as if to say, "Hey! Remember me?" Storm's behavior breaks the cycle of panic, bringing Buss back to the present and thereby stopping the escalation of anxiety before it becomes a full-blown panic attack or flashback. "He's my best friend, and I put a lot of trust in that," says Buss. "I trust him not to mislead me, not to

Storm is by Jerry's side to ensure that Jerry can accomplish whatever he needs to do.

Jerry makes sure that Storm gets down time, and, like any retriever, Storm can't get enough of the water.

let me go where I shouldn't. I know he won't let me go there—to a bad place."

Due to an injury unrelated to his military service, Buss uses a wheelchair full-time to get around. Storm has also been trained to help mitigate Buss's mobility issues and help Buss perform tasks, such as retrieving clothes and shoes and getting dressed and undressed, that most people take for granted. Storm also retrieves remote controls, cell phones, keys, credit cards, eyeglasses, and other items that Buss drops or can't reach. He's trained to tug open and push closed the refrigerator door and to close household doors; he can't open some doors because of the round knobs, but he can push them closed. Because of Storm's

Storm uses a rope to pull open the refrigerator door.

training, Buss no longer relies as much on his private-duty nurse or others to help him perform his daily tasks.

Being together twenty-four hours a day, seven days a week, Buss couldn't help but teach Storm a few additional skills. "I taught him to retrieve laundry from the washing machine and hand it to me so I can put it in the dryer," says Buss. "It's a stackable washer and dryer, and he can't reach [the dryer]."

The only time that Buss and Storm are apart is when Storm goes to the groomer. "He loves to have his toenails cut," says Buss. "It's the funniest thing ever. He just sticks his paw out and waits for them to be clipped."

Although it might seem like all work and no play for Storm, Buss regularly takes him to a private pool to swim, play, burn off stress, and be a dog. And, like a true retriever, Storm loves swimming and retrieving. "He'd stay in the pool all day if I let him." Beautiful, intelligent, and very talented, it is no surprise that the Golden Retriever remains one of the most versatile dog breeds working today, and one of the most utilized breeds for service-dog work.

As a PTSD-trained service dog, Storm helps Buss navigate while out in public. "He's like my army buddy," says Buss. "He's always watching out for me. We have a covalent bond. An unbreakable bond. I trust him with my life."

May 15, 2015, marked yet another milestone in their tale of success and a major breakthrough for Buss. With Storm by his side, Buss drove for the first time in more than three years. "It's not that I couldn't drive; I didn't have the confidence to drive," says Buss. "Storm gave me back my confidence." It wasn't a long drive—only 20 miles or so—but it was a huge milestone in this veteran's forty-year journey back from the Vietnam War.

Storm was named after General "Stormin'" Norman Schwarzkopf, United States Army.

INDEX

Photo Credits